CONTENTS

HITLER'S WAR MACHINE

PANZER
COMBAT REPORTS

Edited and Introduced by
Bob Carruthers

Pen & Sword
MILITARY

This edition published in 2013 by
Pen & Sword Military
An imprint of
Pen & Sword Books Ltd
47 Church Street
Barnsley
South Yorkshire
S70 2AS

First published in Great Britain in 2011 in digital format by
Coda Books Ltd.

Copyright © Coda Books Ltd, 2012
Published under licence by Pen & Sword Books Ltd.

ISBN 978 1 78159 212 0

A CIP catalogue record for this book is
available from the British Library

Printed and bound by CPI Group (UK) Ltd, Croydon, CR0 4YY

Pen & Sword Books Ltd incorporates the Imprints of Pen & Sword Aviation, Pen &
Sword Family History, Pen & Sword Maritime, Pen & Sword Military, Pen & Sword
Discovery, Pen & Sword Politics, Pen & Sword Atlas, Pen & Sword Archaeology,
Wharncliffe Local History, Wharncliffe True Crime, Wharncliffe Transport, Pen & Sword
Select, Pen & Sword Military Classics, Leo Cooper, The Praetorian Press, Claymore
Press, Remember When, Seaforth Publishing and Frontline Publishing

For a complete list of Pen & Sword titles please contact
PEN & SWORD BOOKS LIMITED
47 Church Street, Barnsley, South Yorkshire, S70 2AS, England
E-mail: enquiries@pen-and-sword.co.uk
Website: www.pen-and-sword.co.uk

INTRODUCTION

ADOLF HITLER was, by nature, a gambler and in the course of a long career marked by a series of calculated risks which spiralled upwards from the gamble of the 1923 Beer Hall Putsch through the carefully measured and successful ventures in the Rhineland, Sudetenland and Austria. The decision to invade Poland was the first in a long litany of mistakes which led to Göterdämmerung, the second main error was the flawed logic which culminated in Barbarossa, the invasion of the Soviet Union, but surely Hitler's biggest mistake of all was to drag a reluctant US into World War II.

Even after the Japanese attack on Pearl Harbour Hitler still had the option to keep the US out of the war, but in a typical act of self-delusion Hitler, on 11th December 1941, declared war on the largest industrial nation on earth. From that moment onwards the fate of Nazi Germany was sealed. It took some months to awake the sleeping giant, but once the US Juggernaut began to roll the end result of World War II was never in question.

While the US was busy assembling its new armies, navies and air forces the US Intelligence Service was already beginning to collate intelligence on its new enemy. This information was gathered and disseminated to the troops who needed it, in the form of two main monthly intelligence bulletins. These were *Tactical and Technical Trends* which first appeared in June 1942 and the *Intelligence Bulletin* which began to appear from September 1942 onwards.

The main focus for the US was initially on the war with Japan and a great majority of the early reports are concerned with the war in the Pacific. However, as America began to come up to speed US forces were soon engaged in North Africa followed by Sicily, Italy and finally Northern Europe. As the war progressed the requirement for good intelligence on the German Panzerwaffe became more and more important, and in consequence there are more and more reports of

German fighting vehicles available to us. The vast majority of those reports concerned the fighting in Russia and it is those reports which form the bulk of what you are about to read here.

The material for the two US intelligence journals was originally collected from British combat reports, German newspapers, captured German documents, German training manuals and Soviet sources. As such the quality of much of what was printed was highly variable, some reports are very accurate while, in others, the precision of the information is questionable to say the least, but that's what makes these reports so fascinating. Regardless of the overall accuracy this is a priceless glimpse into how the men in the front lines learned about their enemy, and as such it presents us with a invaluable insight into the events of the Eastern Front were perceived at the time when they actually unfolded. The reports also provide us with a host of information concerning the minor aspects of the thousands of tactical combats being waged day in and day out which expand our knowledge of the realities of the fighting in Russia.

Thank you for buying this book. I hope you enjoy reading these long forgotten reports as much as I enjoyed discovering them and collating them for you. Other volumes in this series are already in preparation and I hope you will decide to join me in other discoveries as the series develops.

Bob Carruthers

1. VULNERABLE SPOTS FOR INCENDIARY GRENADES ON GERMAN TANKS

Tactical and Technical Trends, No 22, April 8th 1943

In attacking enemy tanks at close quarters with Molotov cocktails or incendiaries, the air intakes are among the most vulnerable points. It is important, therefore, that the location of these intakes and outlets be known, as the flame and fumes of a grenade thrown against an intake while the engine is running will be sucked inside, but if the grenade lands on an outlet, they will be blown clear of the tank.

The best targets are the flat top-plates behind the turret. Side intakes are invariably protected by a vertical baffle. The accompanying sketches show the "soft spots" in German tanks Pz.Kw. 2, 3, and 4.

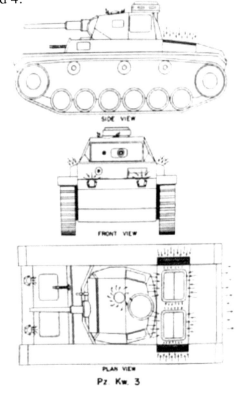

SIDE VIEW

FRONT VIEW

PLAN VIEW
Pz. Kw. 3

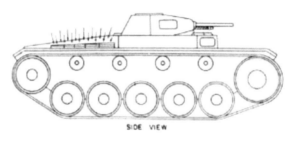

SIDE VIEW

PLAN VIEW

Pz. Kw. 2

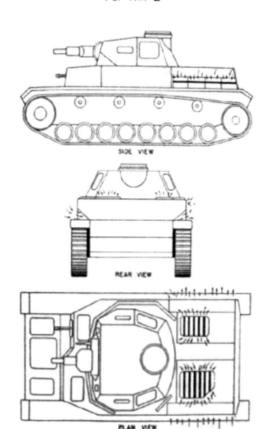

SIDE VIEW

REAR VIEW

PLAN VIEW

Pz. Kw. 4

9

2. OBSOLETE GERMAN TANKS

Handbook on German Military Forces, March 1945

a. GENERAL.

The Pz. Kpfw. I, Pz. Kpfw. II, and Pz. Kpfw. III, although obsolete, are discussed here since they still may be met occasionally in the field.

b. LIGHT TANK (Pz. Kpfw. I).

(1) General. This was the first tank to be standardized by the Germans, and the first ones were produced in 1934. Three models (A, B, and C) and a commander's version (based on model B) have been identified, but model C never has been encountered in action. The hull of the Pz. Kpfw. I was used as a self-propelled mount for several types of artillery weapons, but it no longer will be met even in this role.

c. LIGHT TANK (Pz. Kpfw. II).

(1) General. This tank is manned by three men: a commander, who acts as the gunner; a radio operator; and a driver. A large number of models of this tank were produced before it became obsolete. In a very much modified form it has reappeared as the Luchs (Lynx) reconnaissance tank in Western Europe. The original experimental models of Pz. Kpfw. II were produced between 1934 and 1936; it finally was abandoned as a fighting vehicle in 1943. A flame-throwing version, Pz. Kpfw. II (F), also has become obsolete and probably will not be met again. Model F, not the flame-thrower tank, was the latest model encountered. The modified hull of the Pz. Kpfw. II is still in use as a self-propelled gun carriage, notably in the case of the 15 cm. s. I.G. 33 and the 10 cm. le. F.H. 18.

d. MEDIUM TANK (Pz. Kpfw. III).

(1) General. This tank has appeared in many models but has retained basic characteristics throughout. The latest models to appear are armed with the long-barreled 5 cm Kw.K. 39 (L/60), which in 1942 displaced the shorter 5 cm Kw.K. (L/42). The original main armament, discarded late in 1940, was a 37-mm gun. The Pz. Kpfw. III now is obsolete and rarely encountered. The excellent hull and suspension have been utilized as the carriage for self-propelled guns, and it is in this form that the vehicle remains in production. The Pz. Kpfw. III has been encountered armed with the short 7.5 cm Kw.K. (the original armament of the Pz. Kpfw. IV), and also as a commander's vehicle, as a flame-throwing tank, as a wrecker tank, as an armored ammunition carrier, and as an armored observation post.

SPECIFICATIONS: LIGHT TANK (Pz. Kpfw. I)

Specification Number *Sd. Kfz.* 101.* (Commander's Model *Sd. Kfz. 265.*)				
Model				
	A	*B*	*C*	*Commander's*
Weight in action (tons)	5.88	6.44	8.96	6.44
Crew	2 men	2 men		3 men
Armor				
Hull front	13 mm	13 mm		32 mm
Hull sides	15 mm	15 mm	25 mm	15 mm
Front glacis plate	8 mm	8 mm		20 mm
Superstructure				
Sides	13 mm	13 mm		15 mm
Turret front	15 mm	15 mm	50 mm	
Turret sides	13 mm	13 mm		
Armament	*Two M.G. 13*	*Two M.G. 13*	One Gun One M.G.	*One M.G. 34*
Dimensions				
Length (feet)	13	14		14
Width (feet)	6.75	6.75		6.75
Height (feet)	5.58	5.73		6.41
Clearance (inches)	9.75	10		10
Road speed (miles per hour)	12	15-16		15-16
Range on roads (miles)	112	87		87
*Sd. Kfz. is the German abbreviation for Sonderkraftfahrzeug, *meaning special motor vehicle*				

SPECIFICATIONS: LIGHT TANK (Pz. Kpfw. II)

	Model F	Model L (Lynx)
Specification number	Sd. Kfz. 121	Sd. Kfz. 123
Weight in action (tons)	11.5	13.2
Crew	3 men	3 men
Armor		
Hull front	35 mm	30 mm
Hull sides	20 mm	20 mm
Front glacis plate	20 mm	20 mm
Superstructure		
Front	30 mm	30 mm
Sides	20 mm	20 mm
Turret front	35 mm	30 mm
Turret sides	15 mm	20 mm
Armament (coaxially mounted in turret)	One 2 cm Kw.K.30, One M.G. 34	One 2 cm Kw.K.18, One M.G. 34
Dimensions		
Length (feet)	14.75	14.83
Width (feet)	7.33	8.25
Height (feet)	6.48	6.58
Ground clearance (inches)	13	16 (approximate)
Engine	6-cylinder, In-line, 133 HP, Gasoline	6-cylinder, In-line, 176 HP, Gasoline
Road speed (miles per hour)	15	40
Range on roads (miles)	118	155

Suspension: Model F: 5 bogie wheels each side quarter-elliptic leaf springing. Front drive sprocket, rear idler.

Model L: 5 axles, torsion bar suspension inter-leaved bogie wheels. Front drive sprocket, rear idler.

SPECIFICATIONS: MEDIUM TANK (Pz. Kpfw. III)

Models L and M	
Specification number	*Sd. Kfz. 141/1*
Weight in action	24.6 tons (approximately).
Crew	5 men.
Armor	
Front nose plate	50 mm.
Glacis plate	25 mm.
Driver's front plate	50 and 20 mm spaced armor.
Hull sides	30 mm.
Rear plates	50 mm.
Turret front	57 mm.
Turret sides	10 mm.
Armament (coaxially mounted in turret)	*One 5 cm Kw.K. 39 with one M.G.34*
In hull	*One M.G.34.*
Dimensions	
Length	17 feet 8 inches.
Width	9 feet 9 inches.
Height	8 feet 3 inches.
Gun overhang	1 foot 3 inches. (approximately).
Ground clearance	1 foot 2 inches.
Performance, Maximum speed	35 miles per hour (approximately).
Road speed	22 miles per hour.
Cross-country speed	10 to 15 miles per hour.
Range on roads	102 miles.
Range cross-country	59 miles.
Trench crossing	8 feet 6 inches.
Step	2 feet.
Gradient	30°.
Fording	2 feet 9 inches.
Engine, Type	Maybach HL 120 TRM.
Fuel	Gasoline.
BHP	296 HP at 3,000 rpm.
Transmission: SSG77 Maybach synchromesh gear box, sliding dog type, manual control. Six forward speeds, one reverse	
Suspension: Six small rubber-tired bogie wheels on each side. Torsion-bar suspension.	

3. TANKS IN THE SPOTLIGHT

Intelligence Bulletin, September 1942

Lately the Germans have been working their Mark IV tank overtime, especially in Libya. It is a medium tank of 22 tons, carrying a crew of five. Armed with one 75-mm. gun and two light machine guns, it has been used chiefly as mobile, close-support artillery in desert warfare. The reported substitution of a more powerful 75-mm. gun may send the Mark IV back to its normal task of serving as the chief element in a breakthrough. Its best possible speed is 31 miles per hour. In studying the photograph for identification purposes, note that the Mark IV has, on each side, eight small bogie wheels and four track-support rollers. Testing a captured German Mark IV tank, the British have discovered that it can be blinded by flame-thrower attack. Although the flames are not likely to enter the turret or the driving compartment, they will coat with thick soot all lookout points, including the telescopic sights on the gun. As a result, the men in the tank cannot fire effectively until they have changed or cleaned their sights.

Mark IV tank

Mark III tank

The Germans also make wide use of the Mark III, a light medium tank of 18 to 20 tons (fig. 3). Formerly it was armed with one 37-mm. gun and two light machine guns, but in most cases the 37-mm. has been replaced by a 50-mm. Its best possible speed is 28 miles per hour, but it is much easier to maneuver on the battlefield than the heavier Mark IV.

The war in Africa has proved, however, that the American M3, known to the British as the "General Grant," has the best tank armor in the world. "General Grants" stay in the fight after as many as eight to ten hits by 50-mm. and smaller antitank weapons. In at least one case, a "General Grant" has continued to perform well after 27 hits. The new American M4, known as the "General Lee," is even more reliable. It has greater speed and more power, and is excellent for reconnaissance and pursuit. Among other improvements, its 75-mm. gun has been placed in the turret instead of on the side. This change gives it an all-around field of fire.

MECHANIZED WARFARE

The tactics used by the Germans in mechanized warfare are of interest to every American in the field. German mechanized tactics are likely to follow certain set patterns. Nevertheless, it must be remembered that German commanders are clever at changing standard tactics to fit the situation at hand.

Under normal circumstances, the first German move is to order armored car patrols, supported by antitank guns, to do a thorough job of reconnaissance. Motorcycle riflemen also lend support if the terrain is suitable. These reconnaissance patrols are drawn from the reconnaissance battalions of the armored division. The size and makeup of each patrol naturally depends on the mission it has to perform. Sometimes the Germans even add a number of light tanks. These reconnaissance detachments not only report our movements and those of their own units, but are supposed to be strong enough to put up a fight, if necessary. While the patrols are trying to find out our strength, German air and ground observers are doing their best to detect our artillery and antitank-gun positions so that these may be dealt with when the main attack begins.

Having decided where to strike, the enemy next brings forward his tanks, supported by motorized infantry. He covers this move by a screen of antitank guns and tries to bring his forward elements, including a company of Mark IV tanks, to within about 2,000 yards of our own antitank guns and artillery. At this stage he generally tries to refuel his tanks under the protection of his forward detachments.

The Mark IV tanks direct their 75-mm. gun fire on our antitank guns and artillery. Meanwhile, Mark III tanks assemble for battle, and often challenge our defended area at different points in strong, close formations.

The enemy then decides where he wants to begin his main thrust. Having done his best to weaken the power of our defense by the fire of his Mark IV tanks and artillery, he opens a strong attack with his Mark III tanks, followed by motorized infantry and guns, and advances on his objective.

In addition, he often directs at least one column (containing tanks, artillery, and motorized infantry) on some important locality in our area, such as a tank repair center. There may be more than one of these thrusts. As a rule, the Germans try to develop them into a pincer movement, with the advance columns pushing ahead to meet at the final objective.

If one of the enemy's Mark III tank columns succeeds in penetrating any part of our defenses and establishing a fairly good position, motorized infantry is then moved forward to within a few hundred yards of the position. The infantry dismounts and goes into action, mopping up as rapidly as possible and organizing the position. German machine guns and antitank guns follow the infantry closely. Every effort is made to turn the captured position into an area, or a series of areas, capable of all-around defense against any form of attack. In this last operation, speed is emphasized.

In Libya, the Germans often start these attacks late in the afternoon so as to have the advantage of fighting with the sun behind their backs. In this theater of operations, the action is usually completed by nightfall. Either side is likely to counterattack soon after dark. Experience has shown that the Germans especially dislike this form of combat, and United Nations counterattacks begun at night have often succeeded in recovering, at small expense, ground lost during the day.

It must be repeated that, although the Germans like to employ established and familiar tactics, they know how to change them when necessary. The best example of this is the new German technique of bringing up artillery in close support of tanks, so that tanks are never required to face antitank guns by themselves.

4. GERMAN MODIFICATION OF FRENCH CHAR B TANKS

Tactical and Technical Trends, No 5, August 13th 1942

It is reported that the Germans are modifying French heavy tanks of the Char B (30-ton) type.

The 75-mm. gun is being transferred from the hull to a new turret. This would be a logical improvement. The gun in its previous position could only fire forward. Moreover, owing to the low mounting in the hull, it could not be fired from the defiladed position, and when crossing antitank trenches the gun barrel was apt to become clogged with earth.

5. GERMAN TANKS FOR USE AS AMPHIBIANS

Tactical and Technical Trends, No 6, August 27th 1942

The German army, during 1940 and 1941, stressed interest in a smooth and steadily increased rate of tank production. Immediately after the occupation of Czechoslovakia, the decision was taken to continue production of the light tank Panzerkampfwagen 38/T, manufactured by the C.K.D. (Ceskomoravska Kolben-Danek) metalworks factory in Prague.

In projecting the possibilities for future use of the 38/T tank (German military marking PzKw 38/T) for amphibian operation, certain new improvements over the older model were to be incorporated into the later type. For example, the Prague manufacturers were told that these tanks must be made waterproof, and provision made for mounting the tank on a floating device to enable the vehicle to surmount waves as high as 13 feet. The maximum seagoing speed was to be 8 miles per hour at least and the tank must be capable of running at this speed for 10 hours. Furthermore, it was to be required that, even while navigating the gun (in a revolving turret) should be able to fire.

A prototype of this amphibian tank, delivered in January 1941, had the following characteristics:

Ability to climb twenty-degree beach slopes was another

Weight	5.5 tons (approx.)
Maximum land speed	25 - 30 m.p.h.
Speed in still water	7 - 9 m.p.h.
Angle of climb (land)	45° slope.
Angle of climb (beach)	30° slope.
Crossing ditch	5 ft. 4 in. wide, 60° - 80° slope on far side.
Armor thickness	0.3 - 0.6 in.
Armament	one 7.92-mm. m.g. in revolving turret.
Power	one 4-cylinder Flatwine motor 135 h.p., rear drive.

specification to be met. There was also the question of finding a way to discard the floating mechanism upon reaching land so that the crew need not dismount. The floating device was to consist of two floats made of balsa wood. The drive afloat was to be provided by two propellers driven by the tank motor through the medium of the track drive sprocket.

There have also been reports that the Germans have been experimenting with a tank capable of crossing the bed of a river. One version is that rubber covers for the turret and guns are fitted for water-tightness, air is supplied to the engine from oxygen bottles, and the crew is provided with oxygen breathing apparatus.

Another version is that the tanks, while under water, obtain their air supply through inlet and outlet tubes connected to a float which is towed by the tank.

Both these methods may be practicable for short river crossings. To travel long distances under water the problem might be solved as in a submarine, but practical difficulties of construction would be considerable if the tanks were required to withstand pressure at more than moderate depths. Also, batteries necessary for long under-water endurance would be very cumbersome and heavy.

6. OPERATING THE MARK IV TANK (GERMAN)

Intelligence Bulletin, December 1942

A captured German training pamphlet contains the following information regarding the duties of the crew of a Mark IV tank, and the means of intercommunication:

1. DUTIES OF THE CREW

The crew consists of five men—a commander, a gunner, a loader, a driver, and a radio operator who is also the hull machine-gunner.

The tank commander, who is an officer or senior noncom, is responsible for the vehicle and the crew. He indicates targets to the gunner, gives fire orders, and observes the fall of shots. He keeps a constant lookout for the enemy, observes the zone for which he is responsible, and watches for any orders from the commander's vehicle. In action, he gives his orders to the driver and radio operator by intercommunication telephone, and to the gunner and loader by touch signals or through a speaking tube. He receives orders by radio or flag, and reports to his commander by radio, signal pistol, or flag.

The gunner is second in command. He fires the turret gun, the turret machine gun, or the machine carbine, as ordered by the tank commander. He assists the tank commander in observation.

The loader loads and maintains the turret armament under the orders of the gunner. He is also responsible for care of ammunition, and—when the cupola is closed—gives any flag signals required. He replaces the radio operator if the latter becomes a casualty.

The driver operates the vehicle under the orders of the tank commander, or in accordance with orders received by radio from the commander's vehicle. So far as possible, he assists in observation, reporting over the intercommunication telephone the presence of the enemy or of any obstacles in the path of the tank. He watches the fuel consumption and is responsible to the tank commander for the care and maintenance of the vehicle.

The radio operator operates the radio set under the orders of the tank commander. In action, when not actually transmitting, he always keeps the radio set at "receive." He operates the intercommunication telephone and writes down any radio messages not sent or received by the tank commander. He fires the machine gun mounted in the front superstructure. He takes over the duties of the loader if the latter becomes a casualty.

2. INTERCOMMUNICATION

The following means of intercommunication are available:

External: Voice radio and key radio, flag signals, hand signals, signal pistol, and flashlight.

Internal: Intercommunication telephone, speaking tube, and touch signals.

The maximum distance for satisfactory voice radio communication between two moving vehicles is about 3 3/4 miles, and for satisfactory key radio communication about 6 1/4 miles.

Flag signals are used for short-distance communications only, and a flashlight is used at night. The signal pistol is used for prearranged signals—chiefly to other arms, such as the infantry.

The radio set, in conjunction with the intercommunication telephone, provides the tank commander, radio operator, and driver with a means for external and internal voice communication. The same microphones and telephone receiver headsets are used in both cases.

When the control switch on the radio is set at *Empfang* (receive), and that on the junction box of the intercommunication telephone at *Bord und Funk* (internal and radio—that is, intercommunication telephone and external voice or key radio), the commander, radio operator, and driver hear all incoming voice radio signals. Any of these men can also speak to the other two after switching his microphone into the circuit by means of the switch on his chest.

For voice radio transmission, the switch on the radio set is adjusted to Telephonic (telephone). The telephone switch may be left at *Bord und Funk*. Either the tank commander or the radio operator can then transmit, and both they and the driver will hear the messages transmitted. Internal communication is also possible at the same time, but the conversation will be transmitted.

If the radio set is disconnected or out of order, the telephone switch may be adjusted to *Bord* (internal). The tank commander and driver can then speak to one another, and the radio operator can speak to them, but cannot hear what they say. This also applies when a radio receiver is available, but no transmitter, with the difference that incoming voice radio signals can then be heard by the radio operator.

The signal flags are normally carried in holders on the left of the driver's seat. When the cupola is open, flag signals are given by the tank commander; when it is closed, the loader raises the circular flap in the left of the turret roof and signals with the appropriate flag through the port thus opened. Flag signals are given in accordance with a definite code, the meaning of any signal depending on the color of the flag used and whether the flag is held still or moved in a particular way.

Pistol signals are given through the signal port in the turret roof, through the cupola, or through one of the vision openings in the turret wall. The signal pistol must not be cocked until the barrel is already projecting outside the tank. It is normally used only when the tank is at the halt. The main function of this means of communication is the giving of prearranged signals to the infantry or other troops.

When the tank is traveling at night, with lights dimmed or switched off altogether, driving signals are given with the aid of a dimmed flashlight. The same method is also employed when tanks are in a position of readiness and when leaguered (in bivouac).

Orders are transmitted from the tank commander to the gunner by means of speaking-tube and touch signals. The latter also used for messages from the commander to the loader, a between the gunner and loader.

7. GERMAN EMPLOYMENT OF TANKS, AND THEIR CO-OPERATION WITH OTHER ARMS

Tactical and Technical Trends, No 7, September 10th 1942

The article summarized below comes from a handbook that is used in the German army, especially by officer candidates. It is called "Tactical Handbook for the Troop Commander" and was written by General von Cochenhausen.

Most of the German tanks are in the "Panzer" divisions, but Panzer divisions are organized in many ways. Some have one and some have two tank regiments. The infantry may be a rifle brigade made up of several motorized battalions, forming a regiment, in addition to a separate motorcycle battalion. There are as many antitank and antiaircraft units as necessary to meet the tactical situation. The whole organization depends on how many men or what equipment is available, on the task to be done, on the terrain and the nature of the hostile defenses.

Generally the Panzer division contains a division staff; a brigade of two tank regiments, each with two or more battalions of four companies each; a rifle brigade of one motorized infantry regiment, which also has a battalion of armored assault artillery and a motorcycle battalion; a reconnaissance battalion; an engineer battalion with combat bridging equipment; a signal battalion; an antitank battalion; an antiaircraft battalion; an artillery regiment; and all the necessary administrative, supply, maintenance, and medical troops.

In order to understand this text it should be remembered that the ways in which the Germans use a Panzer division vary according to the mission, the commander's conception of the terrain, and the nature of the hostile defenses.

TRANSLATION

"The entire force of our troops is concentrated in the attack" — Frederick the Great

1. PREPARATION FOR THE ATTACK.

a. General.

The time before an attack should be spent in studying the terrain, preparing positions, and making arrangements to work with the other arms. The study of the terrain should cover the area from the assembly position forward to the front line, and then as far as possible into the enemy's position. The tank force commander, or an officer chosen by him, should take part in this study. Aerial photographs should be used along with the map. It is important to find out the location of mines and the position of the enemy's defense weapons.

b. Surprise.

Surprise is most important for a successful attack. Therefore, all preparations must be carefully camouflaged. Tank units should move at night, and in the daytime they should move only when they can be hidden from enemy airplanes. The time of the tank attack must be set so that it will come as a surprise. The enemy can be kept from knowing that an attack is coming by engaging him in a few local actions, as well as by camouflaging our radio communications or by keeping the radio silent.

c. Organization of the Tank Force.

The tank force commander must decide in every case whether he is going to attack with his tanks in line or in column. An attack in column facilitates control, and makes it possible to maneuver tanks in any direction; to attack in line makes the enemy stretch out his defense, and supports the infantry attack over a broader front.

d. Objectives.

Tanks set out to attack the enemy's infantry and infantry heavy weapons, artillery, command posts, reserves, and rear communications. But before they can get through to these targets, they must destroy their most dangerous enemy, the antitank defenses. For this reason the heaviest and most powerful tanks must lead the attack, and they must be supported by the other arms, both before and during the attack.

Only after the antitank defenses have been destroyed can the tanks go ahead. After that, the most powerful tanks should be directed to attack the points that are deepest within the enemy positions, such as artillery, reserves, and command posts. The lighter tanks attack the infantry. Each echelon of tanks should be definitely informed concerning its mission and its objective.

Tank forces are also able to seize important points, such as river crossings, and to hold them until the infantry comes up.

e. Assembly Positions.

The Panzer division usually prepares for an attack in a position, not too near the battlefield, which gives cover against observation and is beyond the range of the enemy artillery. Here the troops should be told what they are to do, supplies should be distributed, and fuel and ammunition issued. If the tank force by itself cannot protect the position, the commander should see to it that the necessary supporting weapons are brought up.

The tanks can go to the attack more quickly if there are several roads leading from the position to the front, and if crossings over railroads, highways, and rivers have been constructed by engineers.

When time is the most important factor, tank units should remain in their assembly positions for a limited period, or they should move directly to the attack without stopping in these positions.

2. SUPPORT OF THE TANK ATTACK BY THE OTHER TROOPS.

a. Infantry. The infantry must direct its heavy machine guns against the enemy's antitank defenses. The other heavy weapons must fire at targets outside the area of the tank action so that they will not disable their own tanks. Signals must be arranged in advance (such as tracers, flags, and radio) so that coordination is assured.

b. Artillery. The artillery fires upon targets in front and to the flanks of the area of the tank action. It fires both high explosives and smoke, and must generally regulate its fire by time. Adjustment can be attained through the radio or the artillery liaison detail, which, riding in armored vehicles, can accompany the tanks.

c. Engineers. Engineers assist the tanks by strengthening bridges, building temporary crossings, and removing obstacles and mines.

d. Signal Troops. Signal troops keep up communications with the commanders, with the artillery, with the services, and with separate units of infantry, engineers, or the air force.

e. Antitank Units. Antitank guns must follow the tanks as closely as possible so as to be able to enter the fight immediately if enemy tanks are met.

f. Aviation. Aviation has two duties: it should serve as reconnaissance before and during the time the tanks are in action, and it should attack the enemy's reserves, especially tanks and antitank defenses, before they can come into action.

g. Rear Services. If a tank force does not have its own medical service, it should be kept in touch with first-aid stations of the assisting troops. During the battle the service troops are held in readiness well to the rear.

h. As soon as the tanks reach their objectives, they at once prepare themselves for a new mission. They send reconnaissance to the front and find out how far the infantry has advanced. They decide their next movement on the basis of these findings.

i. After the battle the tank force is withdrawn behind the lines and reorganized. The longer it has been in action, the longer the rest period should be.

3. EXAMPLES OF COMBAT ORDERS AND OPERATIONS.

a. General. Orders to the tank force must be kept brief and simple in all situations during a war of movement. It is enough if they tell: (1) the location and strength of the enemy; (2) the location and mission of our own troops; (3) the mission for the tank force, to include direction of attack, the objective, and sometimes the hour the tanks are to attack and their action after the attack; and (4) what support is to be given by other arms.

Example No. 1 (see figure No. 1) illustrates an order to a Panzer detachment in the advance.

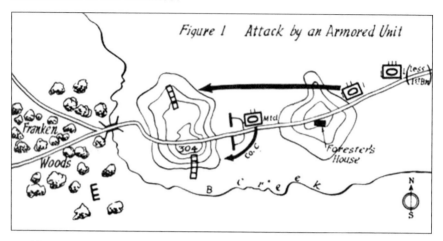

Figure 1   Attack by an Armored Unit

(1) **The Order.** The Motorcycle Battalion has encountered the enemy and has deployed on each side of the road in front of Hill 304.

The commander of the 1st Battalion, 1st Panzer Regiment, meets the commander of the advance guard (probably the motorcycle battalion commander) at the forester's house. After receiving brief information about the terrain, he issues the following order:

"The enemy holds Hill 304. Hostile artillery, estimated to be one battery, is firing from the direction south of Franken Woods.

"The Motorcycle Battalion deploys for attack on both sides of the road. Company C is advancing here left of the road against the southern edge of Hill 304.

"The 1st Battalion, moving north of the road, will attack Hill 304. After overcoming the resistance thereon, it will continue across B Creek to attack the enemy artillery south of Franken Woods. It will continue combat reconnaissance to the far end of Franken Woods. I want to know:

a. When the crossing over B Creek begins.

b. When the hostile artillery has been reached and overcome."

(2) **The Engagement.** The commander of the 1st Battalion then drives to the commander of Company A and orders him to advance

around the northern edge of the woods just in front of him and to attack Hill 304. He then gives the necessary commands to the other companies by radio.

While Company A is deploying, Company B, with its left flank on the road, advances against Hill 304. Company D supports the attack from the vicinity of the forester's house. Company C, forming the second line, follows Companies A and B, and the Battalion commander advances with it. As soon as Company A reaches Hill 304, Company D begins to displace forward to this position.

Meantime, the artillery has been definitely located south of Franken Woods. The Battalion commander now issues a new order to attack the artillery and Companies A, B, and D proceed around Hill 304. Company C then engages the remaining resistance on Hill 304 until the motorcyclists come up from the south side. A part of Company A carries out the reconnaissance on the far side of Franken Woods.

c. Attack Against a Prepared Position. If the tanks are to attack a prepared defensive position, the commander of the force must then coordinate all the arms in his command to assist the tanks. Therefore, every arm must be told exactly what to do in an action which is intended first of all to support the tanks against the enemy's antitank weapons.

(1) Preparation. The commander tells the tank force commander about such matters as the enemy, the terrain, and the plan of attack. The tank force commander reports the results of his own reconnaissance, how he thinks the attack should be carried out, and what sort of support he wants. The commander then makes his decision and draws up the order. The tank force commander then informs his subordinates about the terrain and what he intends to do. The tank forces advance to the assembly position on the roads that the commander has assigned to them. These roads are kept free of other troops.

(2) The Tank Force Combat Order. The order should contain:

(a) Information about the enemy (his position, strength, and the location of known or suspected antitank weapons) and the position of our troops. All later messages from the front that contain information for the tanks are passed on at once to the tank force commander.

(b) Our own intentions, stated thus:

"Tank force — in —, echelons — at (time) crosses the front line, attacks with the first echelon across —, toward —, advancing thence to —. The second echelon attacks —. After the attack the tanks will —. (This order should give the mission and support furnished by the infantry, if a part of the tank force is not placed directly under an infantry unit or attached to it.)

(c) Artillery —. Smoke —.

(d) Engineers —.

(e) Aviation —.

(f) Signal Communications —.

(g) Rear Services —.

(h) Command post of the higher commander is at — (where reports are to be sent).

d. Example No. 2 (see Figure No. 2) illustrates a typical problem for the cooperation of tanks with other arms.

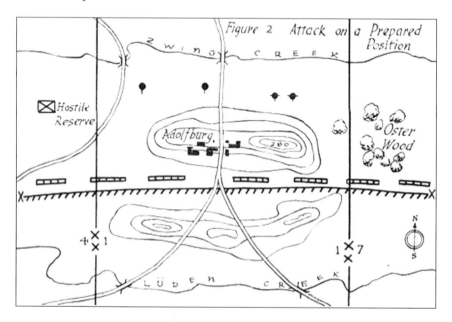

Figure 2   Attack on a Prepared Position

(1) **Situation.** An infantry division, encountering increasing hostile resistance, arrived at the line X — X at 1600 hours. The division, supported by the Panzer Brigade, will renew the attack the next morning.

(2) **Operations**. In the morning, after a brief artillery bombardment, the widely deployed tanks break into the enemy line. The infantry push through the break. Meantime, the artillery advances its fire to the village, Adolfburg, and the Zwing Creek crossings. Smoke troops place fire on the western edge of Oster Wood. Wherever the enemy's antitank weapons are found, they are immediately engaged by heavy infantry weapons and by the tanks. Heavy artillery fire is kept up on Adolfburg. The first echelon of tanks is now advancing rapidly north around both sides of the village; the second echelon decreases its speed and attacks the enemy forces still resisting on the high ground on both sides of Adolfburg. The artillery constantly moves its fire forward so as not to hinder the advancing tanks, being informed by its own forward observers who advance with the leading tanks.

On the right, the infantry attack in the direction of Oster Wood has been checked. Guided to the place by tracers and flag signals, the second echelon of tanks moves toward Oster Wood. Meantime the commander of the first echelon reports:

"Have overcome hostile artillery groups north of Adolfburg.
Am continuing toward the artillery discovered farther west.
Reconnaissance toward Zwing Creek reports that the stream is passable."

The supporting infantry has been mopping up Adolfburg and the high ground on both sides of the town. This infantry now proceeds to assist the tanks at Oster Wood. Then the heavy weapons and artillery are brought forward to Adolfburg. The enemy, retreating along the road, offers stubborn resistance, but is overcome by elements of the tank battalion cooperating with the advance infantry. Zwing Creek crossings are kept under the fire of tanks, artillery, and combat aviation.

END OF TRANSLATION

COMMENT:

1. These instructions show how much emphasis the Germans put upon surprise, which is even more important in an attack by tanks than in an infantry attack. Speed is necessary, and so is concealment, but careful preparations are not to be neglected. The approaches are carefully selected, traffic regulations worked out, and reconnaissance and engineer units make every effort to secure quick, unbroken movement of the tanks from the assembly position into combat. The supply system is planned to avoid delay. Because the Germans are well trained, these arrangements are executed in a businesslike manner, which makes them look simple and easy, though they are often difficult and complicated.

2. German tank attacks are based upon an accurate estimation of the opposing strength and defenses, and the organization of their attacking force is determined by the situation. The tanks leave the assembly position in the formations they will hold during the attack. In difficult terrain, the detailed deployments are made just behind the last cover before coming into the open. Careful scouting of the position, studies of maps and photographs, the planned removal of obstacles, and the preparation of material to be used in negotiating unforeseen obstacles enable the tanks to come upon the enemy with surprise and with a mass fire effect.

3. The heavy tanks attack first to clear the way for the lighter tanks, which then operate against any resistance likely to hold up the infantry. The Germans realize that tanks must act in close cooperation with infantry, but at the same time they believe that the tanks should be free to strike hard by themselves. Therefore they plan things so that each tank unit has a definite goal to reach.

4. German artillery gives the tanks good support; to work out this support, artillery officers ride in the tanks and signal the ranges to the guns.

5. The Germans regard the tank as the decisive weapon and arrange for its support by all other arms.

6. Note in Example No. 1 of the combat orders that the tank battalion commander does not waste time by getting together his

subordinates and issuing a complete order. Instead, he gives his order orally to the officers near at hand, and to the others by radio. What looks at first like a piecemeal action is actually a united effort by the entire battalion.

7. In Example No. 2 note that smoke was used along the edge of the woods; where hostile antitank and other weapons, even if observed, would be difficult to combat with tanks.

8. German antitank crews are trained to be ready for action at any moment and to fire very rapidly.

9. Not only are the tank units supported by the other arms, but the German tank units support each other. Individual tanks within the platoon, and platoons within the company, will fire while halted in concealment in order to protect other tanks or platoons advancing to positions from which they in turn will be able to protect their former supporting group.

8. GERMAN 75-MM ASSAULT GUN

Tactical and Technical Trends,
No 7, September 10th 1942

This assault gun is a self-propelled gun mounted on a standard Mark III tank chassis. In 1940 a relatively small number took part in the Battle of France and it was first used extensively in the summer of 1941, when it played an important tactical role in the first battles on the Russian front.

The guns are organized into independent battalions, although it is now possible that they are organic within the motorized and Panzer divisions and are attached to front-line infantry divisions. Normally only direct fire is used.

An assault gun captured in the Middle East is described below.

The gun and mount weigh about 20 tons.

The gun itself is the short-barreled 75-mm tank gun originally mounted in the Mark IV tank. The range drum is graduated for HE up to 6,550 yards and for AP up to 1,640 yards. Elevation and traverse are hand-operated. Some other details are these:

Length of Bore	23.5 cals.
Muzzle velocity (estimated	1,600 f.s.
Elevation	20°
Depression	5°
Traverse	20°
Weight of Projectiles	
HE	12 lb. 9 oz.
Smoke	13 lb. 9 oz.
AP (with ballistic cap)	13 lb. 9 oz.
AP (hollow charge)	not known
Estimated penetration of AP (with ballistic cap)	55 mm (2.16 in.) at 60° at 400 yds.

It is believed that this low-velocity gun is being replaced by a high-velocity 75-mm gun with a reported length of bore of about

43 calibers. The Germans are also apparently making a similar change in the armament of the Mark IV Tank.

As stated above, the hull is that of the standard German Mark III tank with normal suspension system. The turret has been removed. The length is 17 ft. 9 in., height 6 ft. 5 in., and width 9 ft. 7 in. In general the armor is 51 mm. (2 in.) at the front and 32 mm. (1.25 in.) on the sides and at the rear. An added 53-mm plate is fitted to the rear of the front vertical plate, apparently between the driving and fighting compartments, and is braced to the front plate by two 31-mm. plates, one on each side of the opening for the gun.

For detailed arrangement of armor plate see accompanying sketch overleaf.

The sides of the hull are reported to be vulnerable to the British 40-mm antitank gun at 1,500 yards, but this gun can penetrate the front only at very short ranges, and even then only the driving compartment.

The engine is a Maybach V-12-type rated at 300 horsepower. The gears provide for six speeds, and steering is hydraulically controlled. The capacity of the gasoline tank is 71 gallons, which is consumed at the rate of about 0.9 miles per gallon at a cruising speed of 22 miles per hour. The radius of action is about 70 miles, the maximum rate of speed about 29 miles per hour.

As in German tanks, this vehicle is equipped to carry extra gasoline in a rack on the rear of the vehicle, which should hold about 10 standard 5-gallon gasoline cans.

The captured vehicle contained metal boxes for 44 rounds of ammunition, and 40 rounds were stacked on the floor at the loader's station. Ammunition is also carried in an armored half-track which tows an armored ammunition trailer. There was also a rack for 12 stick grenades, and the usual smoke-candle release mechanism for 5 candles was fitted to the rear. For communication there were two radio receivers and one transmitter. For observation a scissors telescope was provided.

As spare parts the 11-mm. sloping plates over the track guard (see sketch) carried two spare bogie wheels on the right side and one on

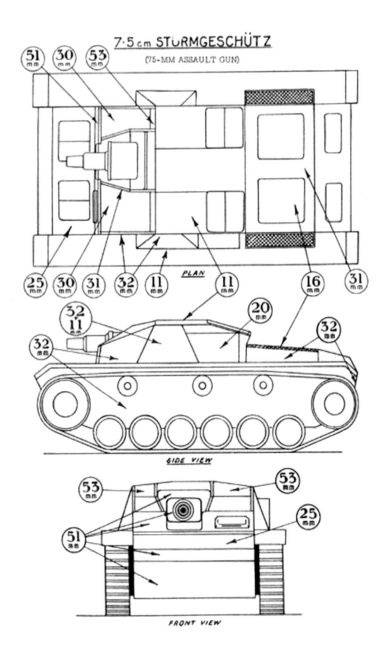

7·5 cm STURMGESCHÜTZ

(75-MM ASSAULT GUN)

PLAN

SIDE VIEW

FRONT VIEW

the left side. Two spare torsion rods were also carried, one in each side of the hull above the bogies.

The crew consists of four men — a commander, gunner, loader, and driver.

9. GERMAN 150-MM SELF-PROPELLED GUN

Tactical and Technical Trends, No 8, September 24th 1942

Reports from the Middle East indicate that the Germans are using, in addition to the 75-mm assault gun (see issue Number 7, page 9), a 150-mm self-propelled gun on a Mark II chassis. Previous reports indicate that an earlier version of this self-propelled artillery consisted of the same gun on a Mark I chassis, but it seems probable that this mount was not satisfactory.

The gun itself is the regular 150-mm heavy infantry howitzer, firing an 80-lb shell a maximum range of 6,000 yards. The elevation and traverse for such a mounting are not sknown.

The armor of the Mark II chassis was formerly about 15-mm., but it is very possible that, plates of 15 to 20-mm have been used to reinforce the front. Details of the armor protection for the gun and its crew are not known. Maximum speed on roads is probably about 24 miles per hour.

10. GERMAN USE OF TANKS

Intelligence Bulletin, December 1942

1. USE OF TANKS

A captured German manual gives the following information about the use of tanks and the support given them by other forces:

a. Tank Objectives

Tanks set out to attack the enemy's infantry and infantry heavy weapons, artillery, command posts, reserves, and rear communications. But before they can get through to these targets, they must destroy their most dangerous enemy, the antitank defenses. For this reason the heaviest and most powerful tanks must lead the attack, and they must be supported by the other troops, infantry and artillery, both before and during the attack. The heaviest tanks should be directed to attack the points that are deepest within the enemy positions, such as artillery, reserves, and command posts. The lighter tanks attack the infantry. Each wave of tanks should be given a specific objective.

Tanks are also able to seize important points, such as river crossings, and to hold them until the infantry comes up.

The tanks can go to the attack more quickly if there are several roads leading to the front, and if crossings have been built over railroads, highways, and rivers.

b. Support by Other Troops

(1) Infantry.—The infantry must direct its heavy machine guns against the enemy's antitank defenses. The other heavy weapons must fire at targets outside the area of the tank action so that they will not disable their own tanks. Signals (such as tracers, flags, and radio) must be arranged in advance so that all units will work together.

(2) Artillery.—The artillery fires upon targets in front and to the flanks of the area of the tank action. It fires both high explosive and smoke. Adjustment can be attained through the radio or the artillery liaison detail, which can accompany the tanks.

(3) Engineers.—Engineers assist the tanks by strengthening bridges, building temporary crossings, and removing obstacle and mines.

(4) Antitank Units.—Antitank guns must follow the tanks as closely as possible so as to be able to enter the fight immediately if enemy tanks are met.

(5) Aviation.—Aviation has two duties: it should serve as reconnaissance before and during the time the tanks are in action, and it should attack the enemy's reserves, especially tanks and antitank defenses, before they can come into action.

As soon as the tanks reach their objectives, they at once prepare themselves for a new mission. They send reconnaissance forces to the front and find out how far the infantry has advanced. Their next movements are decided on the basis of these findings.

After the battle the tank force is withdrawn behind the lines and reorganized. The longer it has been in action, the longer the rest period should be.

11. 75-MM ASSAULT ARTILLERY

Intelligence Bulletin, July 1943

The German 75-mm assault gun is a weapon comparable to the U. S. 75-mm and 105-mm self-propelled guns. The gun and mount weigh about 20 tons. The maximum speed across country is about 7 miles per hour; on roads, about 22 miles per hour. It can average about 15 miles per hour. On normal roads its radius of action is about 100 miles; across country, about 50 miles. To move an assault-gun battery 100 kilometers (about 65 miles) requires 4,000 liters (about 1,050 gallons) of gasoline. The range of the 75-mm short-barreled tank gun, with which this weapon was originally equipped, is about 6,000 yards.

Apparently there are now three types of German assault guns in service: the short-barreled 75-mm tank gun, with a bore 23.5 calibers in length; the long-barreled 75-mm tank gun, with a bore 43 calibers in length; and an intermediate gun which seems to be a 75-mm gun with a bore 30 calibers in length. It seems probable that the long-barreled 75, which is the principal armament of the new Pz. Kw. 4 tank, may be primarily an antitank weapon, while the intermediate gun will take the place of the old short-barreled 75 as a close-support weapon.

A 1940 German document states that the assault gun "is not to be used for antitank purposes, and will only engage enemy tanks in self-defense or where the anti-tank guns cannot deal with them." However, a 1942 German document states that "the assault gun may be used successfully against armored vehicles and light and medium tanks." This apparent contradiction can perhaps be explained by the fact that prior to the invasion of Russia in 1941, this weapon had been used in limited numbers. Experience in Russia may have shown that it could be used successfully against tanks, although Russian sources refer to it as an infantry support weapon, essentially. Perhaps a more logical explanation lies in two German technical developments since 1940, namely: hollow-charge ammunition, which is designed to achieve good armor-piercing performance at relatively low muzzle velocities, and the reported replacement of the short-barreled, low-velocity 75-mm with the long-barreled, high-velocity 75-mm gun on some of the newer models.

The following information about German assault artillery is a condensation of a recent article in "Red Star," the official Soviet Army publication, and deals with only one of the three types—the short-barreled 75-mm.

The Germans make extensive use of self-propelled guns as assault artillery. Their most important mission is to destroy the opposition's antitank and heavy infantry weapons. The German self-propelled mount under discussion is a Pz. Kw. 3 chassis armed with a short-barreled 75-mm gun, which has a semiautomatic breech block. The gun's traverse is limited. The armor on the front and sides of the vehicle has thicknesses of 50 mm and 30 mm, respectively. The top and rear of the gun carriage is open. The speed of the self-propelled gun is about 31 miles per hour, and its range is about 84 miles. The gun's initial muzzle velocity is about 1,389 feet per second. The gun carries 56 rounds. The ammunition is fixed and consists of the following types: high-explosive, armor-piercing, and smoke.

The gun crew consists of a gun commander, a gunner, a loader, and a driver. Two self-propelled guns make up a platoon. The platoon commander's vehicle is equipped with signal flags, rocket pistols, a two-way radio, and a speaking tube for communication between the commander and his gunner and driver. The radius of the radio is about 2 1/2 miles when the vehicle is at the halt, and from 1 1/4 to a little less than 2 miles when it is moving. The second vehicle in the platoon has only a receiving set and signal flags.

There are three platoons in a battery, as well as a separate gun for the battery commander, three armored vehicles with supplies, and an ordinary supply truck. In a battalion (the largest unit) there is a headquarters, a headquarters battery, and three firing batteries. The battalion commander has a gun under his own personal command. According to the German table of organization, the battalion of assault guns is an independent unit and is part of the GHQ artillery pool. The assault artillery battalion can be placed under the command of an infantry commander or tank unit commander, but not under an officer of lower rank than regimental commander. It is important to note that if an assault-gun battery has the necessary supplies to permit it to take care of itself, it may assume an independent role, apart from that of the battalion.

Assault batteries, which are assigned a limited number of targets, have the mission of supporting the attacks of the infantry, and of destroying the opposition's heavy infantry weapons and strong points disclosed during the course of the attack. In supporting tank attacks, the self-propelled artillery assumes some of the normal tasks of the heavier tanks, including the destruction of antitank guns.

The assault artillery never serves as antitank artillery in an attack; only in self-defense does it open fire at short range, shooting armor-piercing shells against tanks. Its shell has almost no effect against heavy tanks.

The battery is part of the combat echelon, and marches ahead of the trains. All seven guns and three armored supply vehicles are in this echelon. In deploying for battle the guns come first, moving abreast toward the front and ready for instant action. The guns of the platoon commanders are on the flanks. The battery commander is stationed to the rear, in a position which is dictated by the type of firing and the terrain. Behind him, the supply vehicles move by bounds from one protected position to another.

If a position lacks cover, these vehicles follow at a considerable distance, maintaining radio communication with the rest of the battery.

In carrying out its special task of facilitating an infantry breakthrough into the rear of the opposition's defenses, the assault battery may follow one of two methods of maneuver: the battery may take part in the initial assault, or it may be held in reserve and not committed until the hostile dispositions have been discovered. In all instances the battery cooperates closely with the supported infantry battalion or company.

Assault guns use direct fire. To achieve surprise, they move forward stealthily. In supporting an infantry attack under heavy enemy fire, assault guns halt briefly to fire on target, which offer the greatest danger to the infantry. The assault guns fire a few times, and then disappear to take part in the battle from other positions. When an assault artillery battalion is attached to an infantry division cooperating with Panzer units in an attack, the battalion's primary mission is to destroy the hostile antitank defenses. If the battalion is supporting tanks in a breakthrough, its batteries seek positions permitting good observation. In other cases each battery moves into the attack after the first wave of tanks, and as soon as the latter encounters opposition, the assault guns cover them with protecting fire. It is believed that the Germans regard close cooperation between the assault battery and the first echelon of tanks as essential in effecting a quick destruction of antitank defenses.

If hostile tanks counterattack, the German antitank guns engage them, and the assault artillery unit seeks to destroy the hostile guns which are supporting the attacking tanks. When the German antitank artillery is unable to stop the hostile tanks, as a last resort, the self-propelled assault guns engage the tanks, opening fire on them with armor-piercing shells at a distance of 650 yards or less.

In the pursuit, the assault guns give the infantry close support to strengthen the latter's fire power.

The most important role of the assault battery in defense appears to be in support of counterattacks. However, in special instances, they have been used as artillery to reinforce the division artillery. When an assault battery is to support a counterattack, it is freed from all other tasks. The battery, knowing the limits within which the counterattack will operate, acts just as it would in supporting an infantry attack. Assault-battery officers and infantry commanders jointly make a careful reconnaissance of the area in which the counterattack is to take place.

The most vulnerable points of a German self-propelled assault gun, according to the Russians, are the moving parts, the rear half of the fighting compartment, the observation apparatus, and the aiming devices.

The Russians contend that their antitank rifles and all their artillery guns, beginning with their 45-mm cannon, are able to fight successfully against the German assault guns. Heavy losses of self-propelled guns, the Russians say, have greatly weakened the German Army's aggressiveness in the attack and tenacity in the defense.

12. TACTICS USED BY PZ. KW. 4'S (WITH SHORT 75-MM GUN)

Tactical and Technical Trends, No 8, September 24th 1942

1. INTRODUCTION

Although recent models of the German Pz. Kw. 4 medium tank have been fitted with a long-barreled 75-mm gun, the Germans are still using Pz. Kw. 4's mounting the short-barreled 75-mm gun (see fig. 1). For this reason the information which follows should prove useful. It is based on German Army documents which discuss the tactics employed by individual Pz. Kw. 4's armed with the short 75-mm gun, by medium tank platoons, and by medium tank companies.

Figure 1.—German Pz. Kw. 4. Mounting a Short-barreled 75-mm Gun.

2. TACTICS OF INDIVIDUAL TANKS

a. Because only a small amount of ammunition is carried, the gun is normally fired while the tank is at the halt, so as to avoid waste. The Germans state that the machine guns mounted in the turret and hull can be employed successfully against mass targets—such as columns, reserves, limbered guns, and so on—at ranges up to 800 yards.

b. As soon as a target has been put out of action, or as soon as attacking German troops are so near a target that it is dangerous for tanks to fire, the tanks move forward by bounds of at least 200 to 300 yards. When changing position, the drivers take care to keep their correct position in the tactical formation.

c. Single tanks may be used for supporting action against prepared positions. The tank normally moves from a flank under cover of smoke. Embrasures are engaged with armor-piercing projectiles, and neighboring defenses are blinded by smoke. Tanks usually do not fire on static defenses at ranges of more than 400 yards. The assault detachments work their way forward under this protection, and as soon as lanes have been cleared through the antitank defenses, the tank follows and engages the next target. The German Army requires close cooperation between tank and assault-detachment commanders. Light signals and other types of signals are prearranged.

The Germans also use single tanks in woods fighting and for the protection of rest and assembly areas.

3. PLATOON TACTICS

a. During the attack, medium platoons move forward in support of the first wave. Half the platoon gives covering fire while the other half advances. The whole platoon seldom moves as a body.

b. The platoon commander directs by radio, and he can control fire either by radio or by firing guiding-rounds to indicate particular targets.

c. Antitank weapons usually are engaged by tanks at the halt. If the nearest antitank weapon can be dealt with by the light tank company, the medium platoon engages more distant antitank weapons or attempts to blind them. Artillery is engaged in the same manner as antitank weapons. The Germans consider enfilade fire especially profitable.

d. If the light company encounters hostile tanks in the open, the medium platoons at once engage them with smoke shells in order to allow the light company to disengage and attack the opposition from a flank.

e. Moving targets and light weapons are engaged with machine-gun fire and by crushing; mass targets are engaged with high explosive.

f. Against prepared positions, the procedure is that described in paragraph 2c, above. When the whole platoon is employed, the advance may be made by mutual fire and smoke support. The platoon assists in the consolidation of a captured position by promptly laying down smoke and fire. Metal obstacles may be engaged with armor-piercing projectiles. The platoon does not move forward again until all hostile weapons in the prepared position have been knocked out.

g. In street fighting a medium platoon may be used in the second echelon to lend support. The Germans employ the tanks' guns in cleaning up nests of resistance in houses; they also use the tanks themselves to crush lightly-built houses.

h. If a front-line tank formation is ordered to hold an objective until the arrival of infantry, the medium platoon gives protection by taking up a position on high ground affording a large field of fire.

4. COMPANY TACTICS

a. Medium platoons under the command of light companies use the latter's radio frequency.

b. Reserve crews follow immediately behind the fighting echelon, and move back to join the unit trains only after the beginning of a battle. They come forward again as soon as the battle is over. Reliefs are supposed to be so arranged that first-line drivers are thoroughly rested when they leave the assembly area to take over before an action.

c. The repair section, commanded by a noncom, travels with the combat echelon until the beginning of the battle.

d. The company commander travels at the head of his company until the leading platoons have gone into action. He then establishes a temporary command post with unimpeded observation of the battle area. Maintaining direction and contact is the responsibility of company headquarters personnel while the commander is at the head of his company.

In the attack the normal formations are the broad wedge (Breitkeil)* or extended order (geöffnete Linie). The Germans believe that effective fire on the part of the whole company can be obtained if the rear elements provide overhead fire or if they fill up or extend the front of their company to form a line.

f. In tank-versus-tank actions, the company is employed as a unit, whenever possible. When hostile tanks appear, they are engaged at once; other tasks are dropped. If time permits, the battalion commander detaches the medium platoons which have been attached to light companies, and sends them back to the medium company. At all times medium tanks attempt to fight with the sun behind them.

g. During the pursuit the medium tank units are employed well forward so that they can take full advantage of the longer range of their high-explosive shells.

5. RECOVERY

Tank mechanics move directly behind the combat echelons. The recovery platoon is responsible for towing away those tanks which cannot be attended to by the repair section. The recovery platoon is under the orders of the regimental workshop (maintenance) company commander, who has under his control all equipment and spare-part trucks of the tank companies. These follow by separate routes as prescribed by him.

* Three platoons are involved, forming a hollow triangle with its apex forward

13. VULNERABILITY OF GERMAN TANK ARMOR

Tactical and Technical Trends, No 8, September 24th 1942

British forces in the Middle East have recently carried out tests with captured German tanks in order to determine the effectiveness of British and U.S. weapons against them.

The 30-mm front armor of the original German Mark III tank (see this publication No. 3, page 12) is apparently a plate of machinable-quality silico manganese. The additional 30- or 32-mm plates which have been bolted onto the basic 30-mm armor are of the face-hardened type. This total thickness of 60 to 62 mm stops the British 2-pounder (40-mm) AP ammunition at all ranges, breaking it up so that it only dents the inner plate. The U.S. 37-mm projectile, however, with its armor-piercing cap, penetrates at 200 yards at 70°. Against the 6-pounder (57-mm) AP and the 75-mm SAP, this reinforced armor breaks up the projectile down to fairly short ranges, but the armor plate itself cracks and splits fairly easily, and the bolts securing it are ready to give way after one or two hits. If 75-mm capped shot is used, however, such as the U.S. M61 round, the armor can be pierced at 1,000 yards at 70°.

Similar results may be expected against the reinforced armor of the Mark IV.

The new Mark III tank has a single thickness of 50-mm armor on the front, and this was found to be of the face-hardened type. The 2-pounder AP projectile penetrates by shattering the hardened face, but the projectile itself breaks up in the process and the fragments make a hole of about 45 mm. The 37-mm projectile does not shatter during penetration, which is secured at ranges up to 500 yards at 70°. The 50-mm plate is softer than the reinforced 32-mm plates being 530 Brinell on the face and 375 on the back. This plate is not particularly brittle and there is very little flaking.

RANGES IN YARDS

	British 2-pdr		British	U.S.		U.S. 75-mm
	Standard	H.V.	6-pdr	37-mm	SAP	APC
Mk. III and IV: 30-mm (old type)						
Lower front plate and turret can be penetrated at	1300	1500	Over 2,000	1600	Over 2,000	Over 2,000
Vizor plate can be penetrated at	1400	1600	Over 2,000	1800	Over 2,000	Over 2,000
Sides can be penetrated at	1500	1700	Over 2,000	2000	Over 2,000	Over 2,000
Mk. IV: 44-mm (reinforced plates)						
Sides can be penetrated at	1000	1200	2000	1100	Over 2,000	Over 2,000
Mk. III and IV: 62-mm (reinforced plates)						
Lower front plate can be penetrated at	No penetration		500	200	400	1000
Vizor plate can be penetrated at	No penetration		600	300	500	1000
Mk. III: 50-mm (new type)						
Lower front plate and turret front can be penetrated at	200	400	800	500	600	1500
Vizor plate can be penetrated at	200	400	900	600	700	1700
Sides can be penetrated at	1500	1800	Over 2,000	2000	Over 2,000	Over 2,000

The ranges at which the different types of German tank armor are penetrated by standard U.S. and British weapons

In tests carried out against the side armor of both the old and new models of Mark III tanks, it was found that this armor showed signs of disking at the back. There is also internal petaling. This, and the condition of the front, which is flaked back at 45° for a short distance, indicates that the heat treatment makes the inner and outer skin harder than the core.

VULNERABILITY OF GERMAN ARMOR PLATE

The Mark IV has only 22 mm of armor on the sides, but this is reinforced by an additional thickness of 22 mm covering the whole fighting and driving compartments. These additional plates are of the machinable type, and the hardness of this plate was found to be 370 Brinell. The bolts holding this extra armor in place are weak, and it was found that the threads stripped easily.

The table opposite shows the ranges at which the different types of German tank armor are penetrated by standard U.S. and British weapons. The angles of impact are determined by the normal slope of the armor on the tank.

14. ARTILLERY WITH A GERMAN TANK DIVISION

Tactical and Technical Trends, No 8, September 24th 1942

The following is a digest of an article written in the Red Star (Moscow) on the use of artillery in a German tank division during attack. It is interesting in that it describes the compozsition of march columns and attack formations, in addition to discussing tactical employment.

The organic artillery with a German tank division, as used against the Russians on the Eastern Front, normally consists of two 105-mm battalions and one 150-mm howitzer battalion, and is usually reinforced by one or two battalions of light artillery.

On the march, the commanding officers of the artillery regiments, battalions, and batteries, plus a minimum of their respective staffs and control units, march at the head of the column. The artillery reconnaissance party marches with the tank reconnaissance unit. Battery reconnaissance parties consist of two armored cars and two motorcycles. In case one of the cars is destroyed the other can carry on the vital reconnaissance work.

Artillery observers ride in armored cars which are armed with machine guns. In each car there is an observer, the observer's assistant, a radio operator, and a driver. There are two such observation vehicles per battery. The battery commander rides in one and another officer in the other. The battalion has three such observers' cars.

Planes are assigned to work with the artillery of the division and are subject to call by the commanding officer of the artillery who assigns through battalion one plane or more per battery, depending upon the amount of planes available. In the attack, one light artillery battalion normally supports one tank regiment in direct support and the medium battalion is in general support. But in the majority of cases experienced, the artillery of the tank divisions has been reinforced so that two light battalions can be assigned to a regiment in the first echelon, which allows one light battalion per tank battalion. One battery of each battalion supports the right element of a tank battalion, another the left element, while the third is echeloned to the rear and is charged with security of the flanks and rear.

Observation posts, command posts, and battery positions are all moved as far forward as possible. Batteries fire from concealed positions, as a rule.

Preceding an attack, preparation fire is conducted from 15 minutes to 1 hour on enemy artillery and tank assembly areas, and observation points are smoked. Enemy front-line infantry is generally disregarded during the preparation, as their neutralization is left to the tanks. Direct-support battalions do not always participate in the preparation fire, but are put in march order with full supplies of ammunition, ready to jump off with the tanks.

The battalion commanders and battery commanders of direct-support units remain at their observation posts in an attack until the head tank passes their line, at which time they take up their positions in the attack echelons. The German general-support artillery does not change its position in an attack which is designed to go no further than the enemy artillery positions. However, in an attack which is intended to penetrate beyond enemy artillery positions, they do move forward when practicable. If the German infantry lags and is finally held up, but the tanks break through and continue forward, the general-support artillery does not move forward.

During the German break-through at the end of October 1941, from the city of Orel in the direction of Mtsensk, German tank units succeeded in breaking through the Soviet infantry lines, but the German infantry supporting the tanks was cut off and forced to dig in. The support artillery could not move forward and, as a result, the tanks, having no support from their artillery, were compelled, after suffering heavy losses, to return to their original positions.

Comment

The above discussion confirms well-known German tactics. It is important, regardless of the success of the enemy tanks in a break-through, to stop the infantry moving up in support of the tanks because the artillery is therefore prevented from advancing and the tanks are deprived of their direct support. The tanks can then be much more easily dealt with.

15. MARK III TANK - THREE BASIC DESIGNS

Tactical and Technical Trends, No 10, October 22nd 1942

Close examination of a considerable number of photographs of Mark III tanks, together with those available for examination in the Western Desert, indicates that the Mark III fighting-type tank is found in three basic designs.

Of these, the first has an armor basis of 30 mm (1.18 in) all around. The front sprocket has eight spokes, and the rear idler, though having eight spokes, is almost solid. This type is known originally to have been produced mounting a 37-mm gun and either one or two machine guns coaxially in the turret, with one machine gun firing forward in the hull. Later, however, the 50-mm was substituted for the original principal armament, and this mounting has only one machine gun mounted coaxially in the turret, the hull machine gun being retained. Of the actual specimens examined, all mounted the 50-mm gun (many are now mounting the long-barrelled type), and in these there has invariably been a Variorex gearbox, the steering being hydraulically operated. This basic type, irrespective of armament, has not been found to carry any additional armor, improvised or otherwise.

The second type has an armor basis of 30 mm all around with additional 30-mm plates bolted on. This type has a six-spoke front sprocket, and the rear idler, although having eight spokes, is more open than the first type. An ordinary six-speed gear box and hydraulically operated steering gear are fitted. Neither photographs nor specimens of this type have shown any principal armament other than the 50-mm gun with one coaxial machine gun. Moreover, every individual tank of this type has had similar additional 30-mm plates on the front and rear, this additional armor not having been found on any other type of Mark III fighting tank. The inference is, therefore, that this additional armor is actually part of the design of the tank and probably incorporated during manufacture. There have been no indications that this type originally mounted a 37-mm gun, although this remains a possibility.

The third type has 50-mm armor on the front and rear, with 30-mm armor on the sides. No additional armor has been found on any tanks of this type, and the armament has always been found to be the 50-mm gun with a coaxial machine gun and one machine gun in the hull. The front sprocket and rear idler are similar to those in the second type, and an ordinary six-speed gear box is fitted, the steering being operated by mechanical linkage. The driver's and hull gunner's entrance doors have been changed from the former double doors to single doors hinged at the forward edge. In place of the normal mantlet protecting the hull machine gun, a more hemispherical mantlet is fitted.

The following minor differences of design between these three basic types have also been noted. Originally on the first type the armor protecting the driver's visor consisted of two plates, one being raised, and the other lowered, to give protection. The third type, and probably the second type as well, have had a single hinged piece of armor which can be lowered to give protection. The third type has also had a slightly different design of the two shields protecting the exhausts from the steering tracks. In the first and second types the air filters were located between the rear bulkhead of the fighting compartment and the engine, air being drawn from the fighting compartment. These filters were believed to be an oil-soaked gauze type. On the third type this arrangement superseded by four oil bath filters, installed over the top of the engine blocks.

The suspension on all these types has been the same, the familiar six small bogie wheels with three return rollers, a front sprocket, and a rear idler. Two early types, however, are known to have had respectively five large bogie wheels and eight small bogie wheels. Both these types mounted a 37-mm gun. Nothing has been heard of either type over a considerable period, and it is probable that they were prototypes only and not produced in significant numbers.

It is known that Mark III fighting tanks have been produced in at least five models designated 'E', 'F', 'G', 'H', and 'J.' These models have consecutive chassis number blocks, and it is logical to assume that they are successive developments. There should therefore be a link with the development shown above, but so far it is not possible definitely to say what each model designation represents. It is, however, known that the first type described above has included Model 'G' tanks, and the third type has included Model 'J' tanks. All three types are known to have been in existence early in 1941, the third type probably being at that time a very new production.

It should be specially noted that, in describing German armor thickness, round numbers are almost invariably given. Careful measurement, has shown that these figures are frequently incorrect. 30-mm, for example, should almost invariably be up to 32-mm.

16. GERMAN TANK MAINTENANCE AND RECOVERY

Tactical and Technical Trends, No. 10, October 22nd 1942

Some of the maintenance units attached to German tank regiments were discussed briefly in Tactical and Technical Trends No. 4, p. 10. More information is now available on these units and is presented here in a summary which involves some revision of the earlier material.

a. Organization

In the German armored divisions, the maintenance and recovery units are ordinarily organized as follows:

(1) Company Repair Section

Each tank company has a repair section consisting of:

- 1 NCO (tank mechanic), section leader,
- 3 NCO's, tank mechanics,
- 13 privates, tank mechanics,
- 2 privates, tank radio electricians,
- 1 private, armorer's assistant,
- 4 privates, chauffeurs.

   Total: 4 NCO's and 20 EM.

This repair section has the following vehicles:

- 1 small repair car (Kfz. 2/40),
- 1 medium cross-country repair truck, for spare parts and tools,
- 2 half-track vehicles (Sd. Kfz. 10) for personnel, capable of towing 1 ton,
- 3 motorcycles with sidecars.

(2) Battalion and Regimental Repair Sections

The headquarters of each tank battalion and each tank regiment has a repair section consisting of:

- 1 NCO (tank mechanic), section leader,
- 3 privates, tank mechanics (for a tank regimental headquarters), or

- 5 privates, tank mechanics (for a tank battalion headquarters),
- 1 private, motorcyclist, tank radio electrician,
- 1 private, chauffeur, tank radio electrician,
- 1 chauffeur.

  Total: for Hq, tank regiment, 1 NCO and 6 men;
  for Hq, tank battalion, 1 NCO and 8 men.

This repair section has the following vehicles:
- 1 small repair car (Kfz. 2/40),
- 1 medium cross-country repair truck, for spare parts and tools,
- 1 motorcycle with sidecar.

(3) Workshop Company

A captured German document gives the following detailed organization of a Panzer workshop company, as of September 15, 1941. It is believed that the organization given in this document is not that of tank units in a particular theater but has general application.

The document sets forth the organization of a workshop company in a Panzer regiment with six companies (as in Libya), but makes provision for added strength (as noted below) in regiments of eight companies, and in regiments of three battalions.

(a) Headquarters Platoon
- 1 cross-country truck (Kfz. 1) — 1 chauffeur, 1 company commander (engineer), 1 officer for special duties (engineer), 1 clerk (draftsman). (One of the two officers may be other than an engineer officer.)
- 1 motorcycle — 1 motorcyclist (orderly).
- 1 medium truck — 1 chauffeur, 2 men for salvaging spare parts (M) [Here, and later, where the meaning of technical abbreviations is not certain, they are given as they appear in the document.]
- 1 light personnel car — 1 chauffeur, 1 official (K-motor transport), 1 NCO for spare parts, 1 clerk (asst. chauffeur).
- 1 motorcycle with sidecar — 1 motorcyclist (orderly), 1 foreman for motor transport equipment (Maybach Specialist).

(b) 1st and 2d Platoons

- 1 motor bus (Kraftomnibus)
- 1 chauffeur, 4 NCO's for workshop service (Vorh.W.=craftsmen?)
- 1 tank electrician and mechanic, 1 tank electric welder, 1 saddler, 1 tinsmith, 1 carpenter, 1 painter, 7 tank motor mechanics, 3 tank transmission mechanics, 1 automobile mechanic, 1 clerk.
- 5 medium trucks, for spare parts and assemblies
- (each) 1 chauffeur, 1 tank transmission mechanic (asst. chauffeur), 1 automobile mechanic.
- 1 medium truck for spare parts and assemblies
- 1 chauffeur, 1 NCO in charge of spare parts, 1 depot chief (M).
- 1 truck with special workshop and trailer for arc-welding apparatus
- 1 chauffeur, 1 NCO for workshop service (vorhandwk), 1 tank electric welder (asst. chauffeur).
- 1 heavy truck, tools and equipment
- 1 chauffeur, 1 tank motor mechanic, 1 blacksmith.
- 1 workshop truck (Kfz.19), with trailer for heavy machine apparatus, Set A
- 1 chauffeur, 1 foreman (leader), 1 turner.

(c) 3d Platoon (Recovery Platoon)
- 1 light cross-country automobile (Kfz. 1)
- 1 chauffeur, 1 officer (platoon leader), NCO (Panzer-Wart, tank mechanic)
- 1 medium cross-country truck (Kfz. 100) for towing apparatus, with rotating crane (3 tons) [A note on the document states that this apparatus will be delivered later.]
- 1 chauffeur, 1 asst. chauffeur (automobile mechanic).
- 1 medium half-track prime mover (8 tons)
- 1 chauffeur, 1 assistant chauffeur (automobile mechanic).
- 2 medium half-track prime movers (8 tons) with underslung trailers (10 tons)
- (each) 1 chauffeur, 1 asst. chauffeur (mechanic), and (for one only of these trucks) 1 NCO (tank mechanic).

- 2 vehicles (with apparatus) [The designation of this apparatus and the vehicle model number are not clear on the original document. The apparatus is designated as not yet available. The vehicles are apparently heavy half-track prime movers.] (6 tons, Sd. Kfz. 41)
- (each) 1 chauffeur, 1 assistant chauffeur (automobile mechanic).
- 5 heavy half-track prime movers (18 tons), with underslung trailers (20 tons)
- (each) 1 chauffeur, 1 assistant chauffeur (automobile mechanic), 1 steerer for trailer; one prime mover has in addition, an NCO (tank mechanic).
- 2 motorcycles with sidecars
- (each) 1 chauffeur (tank mechanic), 1 NCO (tank mechanic). (One of the NCO's is second in command.)

(d) Armory Section

- 1 medium cross-country automobile (Kfz. 15 m.G.)
- 1 chauffeur, 2 armorers (one is section leader), 1 armorer's helper.
- 1 motorcycle with sidecar
- 1 NCO armorer (0), 1 helper.
- 3 vehicles (not described), for armorer's tools
- One with 1 chauffeur, 1 NCO, armorer (0), 1 tank electrician and mechanic (asst. chauffeur);
- One with 1 chauffeur, 1 tank electrician (asst. chauffeur), 1 armorer's helper;
- One with 1 chauffeur, 2 armorer's helpers (one is asst. chauffeur).
- 1 light cross-country car for supply of tools
- 1 chauffeur, 1 armorer's helper.

(e) Workshops for Communications Equipment

- 1 battery-charging truck (Kfz. 42) [According to the document, there is a trailer attached to this truck, but no description is given.]
- 1 chauffeur, 1 NCO mechanic (leader), 1 mechanic.

- 1 communications workshop truck (Kfz. 42) [An ambiguous note suggests that this equipment had not yet been delivered.]
- 1 chauffeur, 1 mechanic (asst. chauffeur).
- 1 light cross-country truck
- 1 chauffeur, 1 mechanic (asst. chauffeur).

(f) Company Supply

- 1 medium truck for rations and baggage
- 1 chauffeur, 1 NCO in charge of equipment (leader).
- 1 motorcycle with sidecar
- 1 supply sergeant (K), 1 clerk (asst. motorcyclist).
- 1 antiaircraft truck (Kfz. 4)
- 1 chauffeur, 1 NCO (in charge), 1 machine-gunner.
- 2 medium trucks for fuel
- One, with 1 chauffeur and 1 tailor (asst. chauffeur);
- One, with 1 chauffeur and 1 shoemaker (asst. chauffeur).
- 2 medium trucks for large field-kitchen stoves
- One, with 1 chauffeur, 1 NCO in charge of rations (asst. chauffeur), 1 cook, 1 asst. cook;
- One, with 1 chauffeur, 1 NCO (accountant), 1 NCO (cook), 1 asst. cook (asst. chauffeur).
- 1 light automobile
- 1 chauffeur (clerk), 1 master sergeant, 1 medical officer.

(g) Total Strength of Workshop Company

3 officers, 5 officials, *[Only one official is designated as such in the preceding breakdown of the company's organization. If the foreman and depot chief in each of the 1st and 2d Platoons are officials, this would clear up the discrepancy.]* 29 NCO's, 158 EM (total, 195 men) and 1 shop foreman for motor transport equipment (group leader).

(h) The document makes the following provisions for enlargement of the workshop company:

(1) For tank regiments with three battalions, add one workshop platoon (same organization as 1st Platoon above). Add to the Recovery Platoon two heavy half-track prime movers (18 tons) with 22-ton trailers, each to have 1 chauffeur, 1 asst. chauffeur (automobile

mechanic), 1 trailer steerer. This involves additional personnel of 1 official, 6 NCO's, 49 EM - total, 56 men. The workshop company then has a total strength of 251 men.

(2) For tank regiments with 4 companies in a battalion (i.e., two battalions to the regiment), add:

- To each of the 1st and 2d Platoons — 2 medium trucks for spare parts, each with 1 chauffeur and 1 motor mechanic (asst. chauffeur).
- To the Recovery Platoon — 1 half-track prime mover (18 tons) with trailer (22 tons), and personnel of 1 chauffeur, 1 asst. chauffeur (automobile mechanic), and 1 trailer steerer.

(4) Light Workshop Platoon

According to pre-war organization, a tank regiment of three battalions had (in addition to the workshop company) a regimental workshop platoon. This unit comprised 1 officer, 2 officials, 3 NCO's, and 48 EM; the vehicles consisted of 1 automobile, 13 trucks (5 to 7 with trailers), and 3 motorcycles with sidecars.

There has been little available information on the workshop platoon since 1940. It is believed that the unit has been enlarged.

A captured document from Africa (1941) gives detailed instructions for a workshop platoon in a two-battalion tank regiment of the Africa Korps (which normally would not have this unit). In this case, an example of the flexibility of German organization, the personnel assigned to the platoon was obtained by breaking up the battalion headquarters repair sections of the two battalions. This workshop platoon was smaller than normal and was to operate, in place of the battalion headquarters repair sections, under command of the regiment.

The platoon was composed of:

- 1 sergeant mechanic (platoon leader),
- 1 Maybach specialist (for engines and Variorex gears),
- 2 NCO's tank mechanics (one an engine mechanic and electrician, the other to be also a welder),
- 2 tank mechanics,
- 1 car chauffeur,

- 2 motorcyclists (mechanics),
- 3 truck chauffeurs.
- The platoon had the following equipment in vehicles:
- 1 light cross-country automobile (for platoon leader and Maybach Specialist),
- 2 motorcycles with side cars (for the two NCO's),
- 1 truck with repair equipment (for 1 mechanic, 1 tank fitter),
- 2 trucks with materials and spare parts (each for 1 mechanic, 1 tank fitter),
- 1 light two-wheeled trailer,
- 1 trailer with reserve of oxygen and acetylene containers.

(5) According to pre-war organization, each armored division had, as part of divisional services, 3 divisional workshop companies. These companies would, on occasion, presumably aid the workshop units of the tank regiments, but information on this function is not available.

b. Functions of Tank Repair and Workshop Units

(1) The repair sections (the available information apparently applies to both types of repair section mentioned above) are responsible for the general maintenance of the tanks, and of their armament and radio apparatus.

In camp and rest areas, they keep a check upon the serviceability of vehicles in the unit to which they are attached; during this period, mechanics are given advanced training through attachment to the workshop company or under master-mechanics transferred to the unit.

On the march, repair sections travel with the tank units and deal with any breakdowns in vehicles or equipment, in so far as these repairs can be effected in less than 4 hours and with field equipment. If a tank breaks down, the repair section leader inspects it and determines the nature of the damage. If the damage warrants it, the tank is handed over to the recovery platoon to be towed away; otherwise, a motorcycle with mechanics stays with the tank to effect repairs, while the other elements of the repair section go on with the column. In this way, one vehicle after another of the repair section stays behind; ordinarily the motorcycles, but, if damage is serious, a half-tracked vehicle. The repair automobile always goes on with the column, while the repair truck always stays with the repair vehicle left farthest to the rear.

In the assembly area, the repair sections thoroughly test all tanks and equipment as to fitness for battle. Any breakdowns are reported at once to the unit motor-transport sergeant.

In battle, the company repair sections are under the order of the battalion commander and are directed by a battalion motor-transport officer. As a rule they follow closely behind the fighting units and range over the battle area looking for broken-down tanks. If the tank cannot be repaired on the spot it is made towable and its position reported to the recovery platoon (of the workshop company).

In one tank battalion in Libya, an armor-repair section was added to the normal repair sections. The personnel was made up of armorer mechanics detached from other repair units, and included an armorer sergeant, an armorer corporal, and seven armorer's assistants. The equipment included an automobile, a motorcycle, and two trucks. This section was to follow the tanks in battle and to work with repair sections on weapons and turrets.

Repair sections are not allowed to undertake the welding of armor gashes longer than 4 inches. In battle, the regimental headquarters repair section is attached to a battalion.

(2) The armored workshop company operates as far as 15 to 20 miles behind the fighting tanks of its regiment, except that the recovery platoon works in the battle area, mainly to tow out disabled tanks.

The workshop company handles heavier repair jobs, up to those requiring 12 hours. Repair jobs requiring up to 24 hours are sent back to rear repair bases.

The workshop company has its own power tools, a crane, and apparatus for electric welding and vulcanizing. Its platoons may be separated, and may operate independently. According to one captured document, a workshop company dealt with 18 tanks in 17 days, under conditions where there was no shortage of spare parts.

(3) The light workshop platoon in the Afrika Korps tank regiment

(discussed earlier) replaced the battalion headquarters repair sections and operated under command of the regiment as a connecting link between the workshop company and the company repair sections. Like the latter, it would handle work requiring less than 4 hours. In attack, this platoon would follow along the central axis of advance, in close touch with the recovery platoon of the workshop company.

The platoon was to carry out work as follows: on brakes, gears, and clutches of Mark II (light) tanks; on damaged gear-mechanism of Mark III tanks; and on valve defects of all types of truck and tank engines except Mark III and IV tanks. They were to remove electrical and fuel-system faults; salvage and tow wheeled vehicles; make repairs on wheeled vehicles; perform autogene welding and soldering work; and charge and test batteries and electrical apparatus.

c. Tank Recovery Methods

All observers stress the efficiency of the German recovery and maintenance units. The following points have been noted:

(1) The Germans will use combat tanks to tow disabled tanks in case of retirement; even during a battle, instances are reported, both from France and Africa, where combat tanks were employed both to protect towing operations and to assist in the towing. The recovery platoon, with its trailers, is not given the whole burden of this main job of salvage.

(2) The same principle of cooperation prevails on repair jobs in the field. Tanks carry many tools, spare parts, and equipment for repair work, and observers believe that the tank crews are trained to assist the repair crews as well as to service and maintain their own vehicles.

(3) Not only is the recovery of German vehicles very efficient, but units will often send out detachments to recover those of the enemy. For instance, a tank battalion may send out a detachment consisting of an officer, one or two NCO's, and six or eight men, transported in one or two cross-country vehicles and protected by one or two light tanks, to search for and recover disabled hostile vehicles.

17. MAINTENANCE AND REPAIR SERVICE IN GERMAN ARMORED DIVISIONS

Tactical and Technical Trends, No. 11, November 5th 1942

The organization of maintenance and recovery units in tank regiments was summarized in Tactical and Technical Trends, No. 10, p. 24. In addition, the German armored division has repair units and workshops which are assigned primarily to the service of the elements in the division other than the tank regiments. However, it is worth noting that some of the divisional repair subsections (see below a. (2)) may include tank mechanics; this suggests that such units may be called upon to assist those assigned to the tank regiments.

The repair services for units other than tank regiments *[These repair units are also found in German motorized divisions, and the scheme of allotment which governs their services applies equally to the motorized division.]* are performed by:

a. Repair Subsections

(1) Repair subsection "a"
- 1 motor transport corporal (in sidecar), leader,
- 1 motorcycle driver (engine mechanic),
- 1 engine mechanic,
- 1 chauffeur (engine mechanic).
- Vehicles: Motorcycle with sidecar, 1 small repair automobile (Kfz. 2/40).

This subsection is allotted to units that have not more than 25 motor vehicles (not counting trailers, or sidecars: 4 motorcycles count as 1 vehicle), except for those units (such as battalion headquarters) which are given repair detachments (see below, b.) The companies in the armored infantry regiment, motorcycle battalion, and the antitank battalion have subsections of this type, as have artillery batteries of all types. *[The sources give the theoretical principles of allotment of repair units; however, it would be dangerous to assume that the scheme is rigorously applied. There is very little difference in size between some types of repair units (especially the repair detachments); furthermore, the Germans make flexible application of any theoretical organization, and these organizations themselves are subject to frequent modification]*

(2) Repair Subsection "b"

- 1 motor transport corporal (in sidecar), leader,
- 1 motorcycle driver (engine mechanic),
- 6 engine mechanics (or tank mechanics),
- 1 electrician (spare chauffeur),
- 2 chauffeurs (engine mechanics).
- Vehicles: 1 motorcycle with sidecar, 1 small repair automobile (Kfz,2/40), 1 medium truck (3 tons), open, for spare parts and personnel.

The principle of allocation of this subsection is not clear from the sources. It is definitely found in the armored engineer company, and may be assigned to the armored radio company of the divisional communications battalion.

(3) Repair Subsection "c"

- 1 motor transport corporal (in sidecar), leader,
- 1 corporal (tank mechanic),
- 1 motorcycle driver,
- 12 tank mechanics (6 are engine mechanics),
- 1 electrician,
- 2 communication equipment mechanics,
- 1 chauffeur (engine mechanic),
- 2 truck chauffeurs.
- Vehicles: 2 motorcycles with sidecars, 1 small repair automobile (Kfz. 2/40), 1 medium truck, for tires and spare parts, 1 medium crosscountry truck, for personnel.

This subsection is allotted to armored car companies in the divisional reconnaissance battalion.

b. Repair Detachments
(1) Detachment "A"
- 1 workshop foreman (official, middle grade),
- 1 corporal (master mechanic and engine mechanic),
- 2 engine mechanics (assistant chauffeurs),
- 1 engine mechanic for motorcycles,
- 1 blacksmith and welder,
- 1 motorcycle driver (clerk),
- 4 chauffeurs (1 is an electrician, 1 an engine mechanic).
- Vehicles: 1 motorcycle with sidecar, 1 light automobile, 1 small repair automobile (Kfz. 2/40), 1 medium crosscountry truck, open, for motor transport repair equipment, 1 medium crosscountry truck, open, for spare parts, tools, and towing equipment.

This detachment is allotted to headquarters of battalions which contain not more than 125 motor vehicles; also, to headquarters of all motorized infantry regiments.

(2) Detachment "B"
As for Detachment "A", except that there are 3 engine mechanics (assistant chauffeurs) instead of 2.

This detachment is allotted to headquarters of battalions (including artillery) which contain more than 125 motor vehicles (examples: motorcycle battalion, armored infantry battalion, antitank battalion, engineer battalion, reconnaissance battalion).

(3) Detachment "C"
As for Detachment "A", except that

(a) There are 5 engine mechanics (or tank mechanics) instead of 2.

(b) There are 5 chauffeurs (of whom 1 is an electrician, 1 a welder's assistant, and 1 an engine mechanic) instead of 4.

(c) The vehicles include an additional open medium crosscountry truck for tires.

This detachment is allotted to headquarters of battalions (including artillery) where the main vehicles of the subordinate units are special vehicles (armored, half track, etc.) and where all the subordinate companies are armored. (The only certain example is the case of the medium artillery battalion.)

c. Special Allotments

One subsection "a" is assigned to each of the following:

Each company of a troop-carrying motor transport battalion (and to the battalion headquarters), motorized bakery companies, and motorized medical companies.

One detachment "A" and two subsections "a" are allotted to the headquarters of the motorized divisional supply services.

d. Workshop Companies

Each armored division *[A motorized division has two workshop companies, organized as those in the armored division.]* has three workshop companies (not including the much larger workshop company of the tank regiment). Each company includes a headquarters, two workshop platoons, an armory section, and a supply section. The personnel totals 102 officers and men (1 officer, 7 officials, 6 NCO's, 88 EM). The equipment in vehicles is 4 automobiles, 16 trucks, 1 half-track vehicle for towing (and personnel), 4 trailers, and 6 motorcycles.

These workshops carry out all motor transport repairs on vehicles sent back by the unit repair subsections and detachments, excepting jobs which require more than 12 hours work. The latter go to base workshops.

18. GERMAN SELF-PROPELLED 150-MM HOWITZER

Tactical and Technical Trends, No. 12,
November 19th 1942

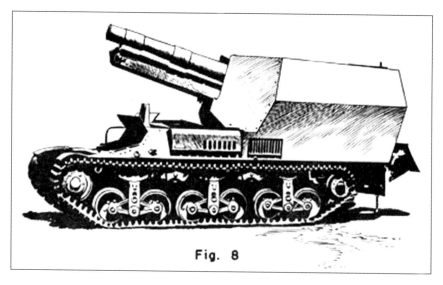

Fig. 8

The 150-mm medium howitzer, sFH 13, has been provided with a self-propelled mounting, the chassis of the French tracteur blindé 38L, made by Lorraine.

The sFH 13 is equipment of the last war, superseded in first-line units by the 15-cm sFH 18. Particulars of the gun are:

Caliber	149.7 mm
Muzzle velocity	1,250 f/s
Maximum range	9,300 yds
Length of bore	17 cals
Number of grooves	36
Elevation	+5° to +45°
Weight of projectile	92.4 lbs

The particulars of the mount 38L are: length, 14 feet; width, 5 feet 2 inches; weight, 7 1/2 tons; engine, 70 horsepower; maximum speed,

22 miles per hour.

The sketch shows the following details:

(a) A fixed gun-house of not very thick plate

(b) A limited traverse of not more than about 4 degrees

(c) A spade on the rear of the hull that can be let down to take recoil stresses.

It is notable that in this case an equipment firing a 92-lb shell to a maximum range of 9,300 yards has been mounted on a hull weighing no more than 7 1/2 tons.

This is another case in which the Germans have utilized a standard field gun to make self-propelled artillery. A recent picture shows another 150-mm howitzer, the 15-cm sIG 33, on a German Mark II chassis with the gun on a special mounting built into the hull. There is a three-sided shield no higher than the normal tank, instead of the very high box-like structure for the self-propelled sFH 13.

19. OPERATIONS OF THE GERMAN TANK RECOVERY PLATOON

Tactical and Technical Trends, No. 12, November 19th 1942

British sources give recent information on the methods employed by the recovery platoon of (tank) workshop companies. This information was obtained from prisoners of war.

The towing vehicles and trailers of the platoon are sent forward to regimental headquarters and operate under its direction.

The principle now used is to have two or three recovery vehicles forward with the fighting units. These vehicles advance in the line of attack and cruise across the width of the battle front. The Germans believe that hostile forces will be preoccupied with the German tanks and will not bother with the recovery vehicles, no matter how close they are.

If a member of a tank crew orders the driver of a recovery vehicle to tow his tank to the rear, the former assumes responsibility for the action—in case it later proves that the damage is negligible and could have been fixed on the spot by the repair sections. However, asking that a damaged vehicle be towed away is always permissible if it is in danger of being shot up.

The towing vehicle usually goes forward alone and tows a disabled tank away by tow ropes. Towing is used in preference to loading on the trailer, as this latter operation may take 20 minutes (regarded by a prisoner as good time under battle conditions).

The recovered tanks are towed to an assembly point behind the combat area, where they are lined up so as to protect themselves as far as possible. Trailers may be used to take back the disabled tanks from this point to the workshop company.

According to this report, however, trailers are being used less and less, and their use is confined mainly to roads. On roads, they enable a higher speed to be maintained, do not weave as much as a towed tank, and do not cut up the road surface. On the desert, trailers would be used on bad ground rather than where there is good going.

The PW's reported that drivers of recovery vehicles did front-line duty for about 8 days at a time; then they worked at the rear, between assembly point and workshop.

20. INCREASED PROTECTION ON GERMAN TANKS

Tactical and Technical Trends, No. 14, December 17th 1942

Recent Middle East reports point out that the Germans are taking considerable pains to provide additional protection for their tanks. Thus far, the measures employed for this purpose may conveniently be considered under two main headings, namely, spaced armor and improvised protection.

a. Spaced Armor

More detailed information than that previously submitted on the Mark III tank indicates the extent to which these improvements have gone. The accompanying sketches, based on actual photographs, illustrate typical arrangements of spaced armor on this tank and throw some light on these developments.

Figure 1 overleaf illustrates the general appearance of the tank when fitted with spaced-armor; figures 2 and 3 are side views of spaced-armor arrangements on the front superstructure and gun mantlet; and figure 4 is a perspective view with the spaced plate of the gun-mantlet assembly removed.

The arrangement of the spaced armor on the gun mantlet appears to be more or less uniform in all the photographs so far received. In all cases the additional plate on the mantlet is curved, as shown in figure 3, and forms the front wall of a box structure, the rear wall of which is constructed of the 50-mm front shield of the gun mantlet, and the sides, top, and bottom are formed by thin sheet-metal plates arranged as shown in figure 4. In one example recently examined in the Middle East, the additional plate was 20-mm thick and was separated from the mantlet proper by an air space of approximately 120 mm (4.7 inches), the air space being somewhat larger than this at the top and somewhat smaller at the bottom.

The spaced armor on the front superstructure is arranged in at least

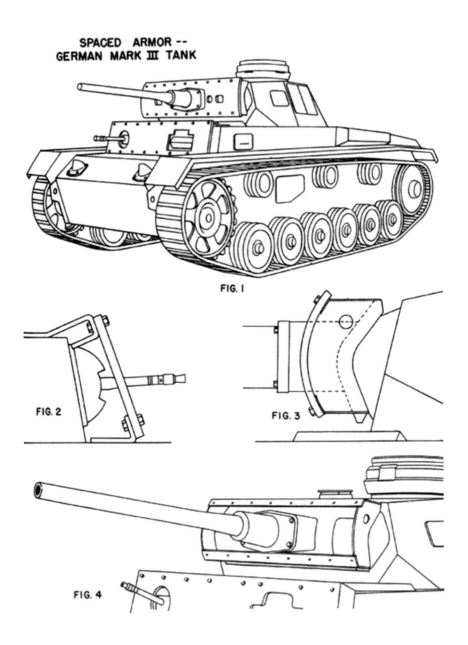

SPACED ARMOR --
GERMAN MARK III TANK

FIG. I

FIG. 2

FIG. 3

FIG. 4

two different ways, the sides for the air space sometimes closed, and sometimes open.

In this tank, the sides of the space between the front of the superstructure and the additional plate were closed by thin sheet metal, the only purpose of which was apparently to keep out the dust. The additional plate was fixed parallel to the 50-mm front plate of the superstructure, from which it was separated by an air space of 100 mm (3.9 inches). It was 20 mm thick and of machinable quality, Brinell hardness tests giving a figure of about 350 on both sides.

In another tank recently examined in the Middle East, the air space in the front superstructure assembly was open-sided. The space plate, which was again 20 mm thick and of machinable quality, was bolted to angle iron supports at the top and bottom; those at the top were welded to the roof of the superstructure, and those at the bottom, to the front sloping top plate of the hull. In this case the additional plate was arranged at an angle to the basic plate as shown in figure 2; the space at the top measured horizontally 108 mm (4.25 inches), and at the bottom 195 mm (7.68 inches).

In every case the additional plate on the front of the superstructure is formed with two openings, one to accommodate the driver's visor and the other for the hull machine gun. It is reported that these openings are such that the fitting of spaced armor does not seriously affect the traverse and elevation of the machine gun and does not in any way impair the driver's vision.

Although, in these two tanks, the additional plate was of machinable quality, a sample from a third tank appeared to be face-hardened, the Brinell value of its front surface being 468, against 359 on its rear surface.

So far, spaced armor has only been reported on the J series Mark III tanks with 50-mm basic frontal armor and the new long 50-mm gun. Since, however, the fitting of spaced armor is probably at present in an experimental stage, it may be found on other models of the Mark III or even on the Mark IV. If it proves a success, it will no doubt be standardized in due course.

b. Improvised Protection

Middle East also reports that German tanks are now frequently provided with improvised additional protection in the form of sand bags attached wherever possible, and lengths of track secured over vulnerable parts. (See Tactical and Technical Trends, No. 13, p. 33).

It is common for some of the sand bags to be arranged on the roof of the superstructure in front of the turret so as to shield the turret joint and the space below the bottom of the gun mantlet, and others around the front and sides of the superstructure. Precautions are taken so as not to obstruct the driver's vision or the free elevation and traverse of the ball-mounted machine gun.

Lengths of track are usually attached across the upper and lower noseplates. They have also been found secured on the front of the superstructure between the driver's visor and the machine gun, as well as draped over the top of the turret and gun mantlet.

The length of track across the lower nose-plate is generally held in position by means of a transverse bar welded to the plate at its ends, while that on the upper nose-plate has been found attached by S hooks to the air inlet cowls of the track brake cooling system.

21. TANK WARFARE IN STREETS

Tactical and Technical Trends, No. 14, December 17th 1942

The following comments were compiled from observations of the recent tank battles in the streets of Stalingrad.

The German commander held the mass of his tanks in the rear areas, throwing only small groups of from three to five tanks down any one street.

The accompanying infantry precedes the tanks, and only when the surrounding buildings are overcome do the tanks advance. Thus, the best defense against tanks in street warfare is to place the most experienced automatic riflemen out in front.

It is necessary to deploy tanks in the defense so that they will form a dense crossfire, enfilade, and flanking fire. This can best be obtained by controlling the street intersections. Infantry and artillery must be disposed in the intervals between, and in front of, the tanks.

It is desirable that tanks held in reserve be assembled near intersections.

Tanks should be controlled by radio. Messenger service is too slow and telephone wire is too easily broken.

The infantry commander must be located near the tank commander, and the commanders of the smaller rifle units must be with the commanders of individual tanks. The rifle commanders locate targets for the tanks, and correct and change their fire from one target to another.

22. ENGINEER SUPPORT OF TANKS

Tactical and Technical Trends, No. 15, December 31st 1942

Experience in Russia and Africa has indicated that tanks cannot operate successfully without the support of other arms. Since tanks have probably been more extensively used on the Russian front than anywhere else, of interest is the following summary of an article from the Russian newspaper Red Star of June 7, 1942, written by a Russian lieutenant, on engineer support of tank attacks on organized defenses.

During the attack, each tank should carry at least 2 engineers. The principal function of these engineers is the location and neutralization of mines. For purposes of coordination, a complete set of visual signals between the engineers (when dismounted) and the tanks must be arranged.

Comment: These engineers apparently ride outside the tank behind the turret. In this connection it should be noted that the turrets of Russian tanks are usually set well forward, thereby leaving a relatively large platform-like area between the turret and the rear of the tank. Some protection can therefore be afforded to men riding behind the turret. The Russians also use infantry mounted on tanks (Desyanti).

23. GERMAN METHODS OF ARMORED ATTACK BY SMALL UNITS

Tactical and Technical Trends, No. 16,
January 14th 1943

The following report is from a lecture by a British colonel who recently returned from the Middle East where he commanded the artillery of a corps in the Western Desert. His lecture was based on both personal experience and intelligence reports.

a. Composition of German "Box" (Moving Defense Area)

The box is the part of the column which is inside the solid line in sketch C. The box varies in size, but if an armored battalion is the basic unit, it might contain the following combat troops, in addition to the service elements:

- One battalion of motorized infantry, usually carried in half-tracked, lightly armored vehicles;
- One battalion of 50-mm antitank guns;
- One battalion of 88-mm antiaircraft-antitank guns;
- One battery of 150-mm close-support infantry guns, sometimes on self-propelled mounts;
- One battalion of field artillery.

On the move or in the attack, the guns within the box are disposed as shown in sketch C. Infantry guns and field guns are usually kept in the box only when the defensive is assumed.

In size, the box is approximately 2 miles deep and has a front of 800 yards. The 88-mm gun, though it has proved a very effective antitank gun, is primarily included in the box to protect the lightly-armored vehicles from air attack.

b. The Method of Advance (see sketch A overleaf)

On very flat country, the distance between the reconnaissance unit

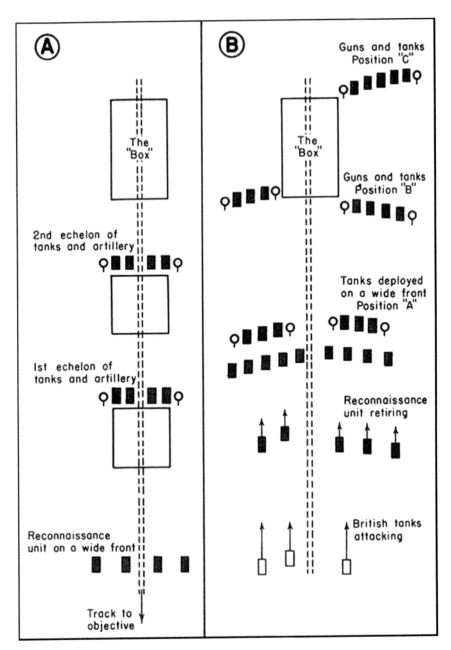

and the leading echelons of tanks is from 5 to 10 miles; the distance between the 1st and 2nd echelon of tanks is 1 mile, and the distance between the 2nd echelon of tanks and the box is 2 miles.

The whole force is directed towards some terrain feature, which, if captured, will force the enemy to fight on ground chosen by the attacker.

Over normal terrain, each portion of the column moves from high ground to high ground by bounds. Each echelon of tanks is supported by artillery which moves in the rear of the tanks.

c. Tactics if Attacked on the Move

When British tanks are reported to be advancing to a fight, the box halts and takes up a position for all-around defense. As the British tanks advance, the reconnaissance units fall back, and the two echelons of tanks deploy on a wide front (see sketch B). If the enemy continues to advance, the Germans continue the retirement to position B (sketch B), and force the enemy to attempt a breakthrough against one of the flanks of the box.

If the enemy decides to attack the German left flank, the troops on the left of the box at position B fall back to position C. The enemy tanks, if they pursue, are then not only engaged frontally by the German tanks from position C, but are caught in flank by AT and AA guns of the left side of the box. Finally, the tanks to the right of the box at position B swing around and engage the attackers in the rear.

If artillery has accompanied the tanks in the advance, it may either continue to support them, or enter the box to stiffen its antitank defense.

d. Attack Led by Tanks Against an Organized Position

In general, the Germans assume that the defenders have seized and occupied the best positions; hence, they attempt to overwhelm him and take over such positions.

The German commander usually launches a frontal attack against one center of resistance. The attack might be developed in the following way (see sketch C overleaf).

Phase I: The German commander will reinforce his reconnaissance unit with tanks deployed on a wide front and drive in the covering force, until the enemy is approximately 2,500 yards from the main line of resistance.

Phase II: A careful reconnaissance will then be carried out by a senior commander in a tank.

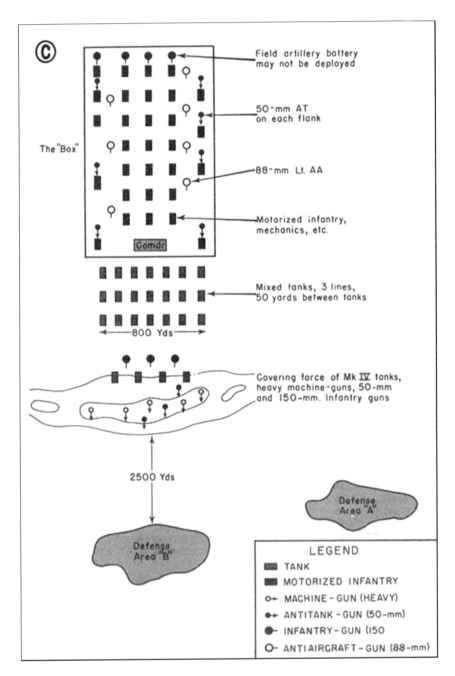

©

Field artillery battery
may not be deployed

50-mm AT
on each flank

The "Box"

88-mm Lt. AA

Motorized infantry,
mechanics, etc.

Comdr

Mixed tanks, 3 lines,
50 yards between tanks

←——800 Yds——→

Covering force of Mk IV tanks,
heavy machine-guns, 50-mm
and 150-mm. Infantry guns

2500 Yds

Defense
Area "A"

Defense
Area "B"

LEGEND

▨ TANK
▨ MOTORIZED INFANTRY
O← MACHINE – GUN (HEAVY)
●← ANTITANK – GUN (50-mm)
●← INFANTRY – GUN (150
O← ANTIAIRCRAFT – GUN (88-mm)

Phase III: The German covering force deploys as follows:

Tanks, generally Mark IV's, take up a hull-down position on a ridge, or high ground, and with the fire of their machine guns attempt to pin down the defenses. They may engage AT guns that are visible

84

with their 75's. Under cover of this fire, 50-mm AT guns, heavy machine guns, and close support 150-mm infantry guns are also deployed in an attempt to knock out the AT guns of the defense, or to kill their gun crews.

Under the cover of fire of this covering force, the attack forms in rear as follows:

(1) Three rows of tanks about 50 yards apart, each row approximately 150 yards in rear of the one in front.

(2) When the tanks are in position, the box forms up in rear as shown in sketch C, the infantry all riding in vehicles.

Phase IV: At H hour, the whole force moves forward at about 15 mph, depending on the ground. As they pass through their covering force, the tanks begin to fire, not so much with a view to hitting anything, but for the psychological effect and to keep the defenders pinned down. On arrival at their objectives, some tanks drive straight through to the far side of the objective, while others assist their infantry in mopping-up operations. The infantry does not usually dismount until they arrive at the objective, when they fan out and use tommy guns extensively.

Phase V: When the attack is successful the covering force moves forward into the captured area to stiffen the defense. The tanks are usually withdrawn and serviced near what has now become their rear area.

24. NEW AXIS SELF-PROPELLED GUNS

Tactical and Technical Trends, No. 18, February 11th 1943

Owing to the battlefield mobility of tanks, as well as to other factors, the towed antitank gun is not always an adequate antitank weapon. To supplement the towed gun, self-propelled antitank guns have been developed and organized into special units: for example, the U.S. tank-destroyer organizations. For a considerable period of time the Germans have shown a tendency to mount a large number of guns on self-propelled mounts, the calibers varying from 20 mm to 150 mm. Recently the following new German equipment of this type was reported to exist:

- German 37-mm AT gun on an armored personnel carrier;
- Russian 76.2 -mm gun on German Mark II tank chassis;
- Russian 76.2-mm gun on Czech light tank (38) chassis;
- German 75-mm tank gun (40) on German Mark II tank chassis;
- German 75-mm tank gun (40) on Czech light tank (38) chassis.

Of the above weapons, the first two are known to have been present in North Africa. Whether the last three have been issued to units is not known. The Germans are also reported to be developing 88-mm and 128-mm armored self-propelled guns.

The Italians are apparently still endeavoring to follow the Germans in the development of self-propelled weapons. It is reported that they now have a 90-mm self-propelled gun. While this gun is known to exist, it is not believed to have appeared yet in action. The Italian 75-mm self-propelled gun (see Tactical and Technical Trends, No. 6, p. 35) is reported to have proved not wholly successful, and it is thought that Italy does not possess sufficient resources to allow free improvisation on the German pattern.

25. TACTICAL EMPLOYMENT OF GERMAN 75-MM ASSAULT GUN

Tactical and Technical Trends, No. 19,
February 25th 1942

The German 75-mm assault gun (7.5-cm Sturmgeschütz) is a weapon comparable to the U.S. 75-mm and 105-mm self-propelled guns. The gun and mount weigh about 20 tons. Its maximum speed cross-country is about 7 mph, on roads about 22 mph; it can average about 15 mph. On normal roads its radius of action is about 100 miles, cross-country about 50 miles. To move an assault-gun battery 100 kilometers (about 65 miles) requires 4,000 liters (about 1,050 gallons) of gasoline. The range of the 75-mm short-barrelled tank gun (7.5-cm KwK), with which this weapon was originally equipped, is about 6,000 yards.

It is reported that there are now apparently three types of assault guns in service. These are: the Stu.G. 7.5-cm K, mounting the 7.5-cm KwK (short-barreled tank gun—23.5 calibers *[Length of bore]*); the Stu.G. lg. 7.5-cm K, mounting the 7.5-cm KwK 40 (long-barreled tank gun—43 calibers); and a third weapon, nomenclature at present unknown, which appears to have a 75-mm gun with a bore 30 calibers in length. It seems probable, therefore, that the 7.5-cm KwK 40, which is the principal armament of the new Pz. Kw. 4 (Mark IV tank), may be primarily an antitank weapon, while the latest intermediate gun will take the place of the old Stu.G. 7.5-cm K as a close-support weapon.

While some technical details of this weapon have been known for some time, relatively little information has been available until recently concerning its tactical employment. Two German documents on the tactical use of this weapon have now been received. One is dated May 1940, the other April 1942. The second document is essentially identical in substance with the first, except that the second contains some additional information. Both documents have been combined into one for the present report, and such apparent contradictions as exist are noted in the translation which follows.

INSTRUCTIONS FOR THE EMPLOYMENT OF ASSAULT ARTILLERY

a. Basic Principles and Role

The assault gun (7.5-cm gun on an armored self-propelled mount) is an offensive weapon. It can fire only in the general direction in which the vehicle is pointing *[Traverse is limited to 20 degrees]*. Owing to its cross-country performance and its armor, it is able to follow anywhere its own infantry or armored troops.

Support for the infantry in attack is the chief mission of the assault gun by virtue of its armor, maneuverability, and cross-country performance and of the rapidity with which it can open fire. The moral support which the infantry receives through its presence is important.

It does not fire on the move. In close fighting it is vulnerable because its sides are light and it is open-topped. Besides, it has no facilities for defending itself at close quarters. As it is not in a position to carry out independent reconnaissance and fighting tasks, this weapon must always be supported by infantry.

In support of an infantry attack, the assault gun engages the enemy heavy infantry weapons which cannot be quickly or effectively destroyed by other weapons. In support of a tank attack, it takes over part of the role of the Pz. Kw. 4, and deals with enemy antitank guns appearing on the front. It will only infrequently be employed as divisional artillery, if the tactical and ammunition situation permits. Assault artillery is not to be included in the divisional artillery fire plan, but is to be treated only as supplementary, and to be used for special tasks (e.g., roving batteries). Its employment for its principal tasks must always be assured.

[The April 1942 document states that "The assault gun may be successfully used against armored vehicles, and light and medium tanks." The May 1940 document, however, states "It is not to be used for antitank purposes, and will only engage enemy tanks in self-

defense or where the antitank guns cannot successfully deal with them." This apparent contradiction can perhaps be explained by the fact that, prior to the invasion of Russia in 1941, this weapon had been used in limited numbers only. Experience on the Eastern Front may have shown that it could be successfully used against tanks, although Russian sources refer to it as essentially an infantry support weapon. A more logical explanation perhaps lies in two German technical developments since 1940: namely, hollow-charge ammunition, which is designed to achieve good armor-piercing performance at relatively low muzzle velocities, and the reported replacement of the short-barreled low-velocity 75-mm with the long-barreled high-velocity tank gun (7.5-cm KwK 40) on some of the newer models.]

b. Organization of the Assault Artillery Battalion and its Batteries

The assault gun battalion consists of battalion headquarters and three batteries. The battery has six guns—three platoons, each of two guns. *[The April 1942 document states that a battery has 7 guns, the extra gun being "for the battery commander."]* The command vehicles for battery and platoon commanders are armored. They make possible, therefore, movement right up to the foremost infantry line to direct the fire.

c. Principles for Employment
(1) General

Assault gun battalions belong to GHQ artillery. For the conduct of certain engagements, battalions or separate batteries are attached to divisions, or to special task forces. The division commander should attach some or all of the assault artillery batteries under his control to infantry or tank units; only in exceptional circumstances will they be put under the artillery commander. Transfer of batteries from support of one unit to another within the division can be carried out very quickly in the course of a battle. Close liaison with the batteries and within the batteries is of primary importance for the timely fulfillment of their missions. The assault artillery fires from positions in open ground, hidden as far as possible from ground and air observation. Only when employed as part of the divisional artillery will these guns fire from covered positions.

Splitting up of assault-gun units into small parts (platoons or single guns) jeopardizes the fire power and facilitates enemy defense. This should occur only in exceptional cases when the entire battalion cannot be employed, i.e., support of special assault troops or employment over terrain which does not permit observation. If employed singly, mutual fire support and mutual assistance in case of breakdowns and over rough country are not possible.

As complete a picture as possible must be obtained of the enemy's armor-piercing weapons and the positions of his mines; hasty employment without sufficient reconnaissance might well jeopardize the attack. Premature deployment must also be avoided. After an engagement, assault guns must not be given security missions, especially at night. They must be withdrawn for refuelling, overhauling, and resupply. After 4 to 5 days in action, they must be thoroughly serviced. If this is not possible, it must be expected that some will not be fit for action and may fall out. When in rear areas, they must be allotted space near repair shops so that they are readily accessible to maintenance facilities, etc.

Troops co-operating with assault guns must give all support possible in dealing with mines and other obstacles. Artillery and heavy infantry weapons must give support by engaging enemy armor-piercing weapons.

Surprise is essential for the successful employment of assault-gun battalions. It is therefore most important for them to move up and into firing positions under cover, and generally to commence fire without warning. Stationary batteries fire on targets which are for the moment most dangerous to the infantry (especially enemy heavy infantry weapons), destroy them, and then withdraw to cover in order to avoid enemy fire. With the allotment of smoke ammunition (23 percent of the total ammunition issue), it is possible to lay smoke and to blind enemy weapons which, for example, are sited on the flank. Assault artillery renders support to tanks usually after the hostile position has been broken into. In this role, assault-gun batteries supplement Pz. Kw. 4s, and during the fluid stages of the battle direct their fire against enemy antitank weapons to the direct front. They follow very closely the first waves of tanks. Destruction of enemy antitank weapons on the flanks of an attack will frequently be the task of the Pz. Kw. 4.

Against concrete positions, assault guns should be used to engage casemates with armor-piercing shells. Co-operation with assault engineers using flame-throwers is very effective in these cases.

Assault guns are only to be used in towns and woods in conjunction with particularly strong and close infantry support, unless the visibility and field of fire are so limited as to make use of the guns impossible without endangering friendly troops. Assault guns are not suitable for use in darkness. Their use in snow is also restricted, as they must usually keep to available roads where enemy defense is sure to be met.

(2) Tactical Employment

Vehicles on the move should be kept well spaced. Since the average speed of assault guns is about 15 mph, they must be used in leap-frog fashion when operating with an infantry division. Crossing bridges must be the subject of careful handling. Speed must be reduced to less than 5 mph, and the assault guns must keep exactly to the middle of the bridge, with intervals of at least 35 yards. Bridges must be capable of a load of 22 tons. The commander of the assault guns must cooperate with the officer in charge of the bridge.

(1) In the Infantry Division

While on the move, the division commander keeps the assault-gun battalion as long as possible under his own control. According to the situation and the terrain he can, while on the move, place one assault gun battery in each combat team. The attachment of these weapons to the advance guard is exceptional. In general, assault gun batteries are concentrated in the interval between the advance guard and the main body, and are subject to the orders of the column commander. *[According to the April 1942 document, the issue is only 10 percent smoke. It is probable that the ammunition issue depends on the particular operations involved.]* On the march, the battery commander and his party should accompany the column commander.

(2) In the Armored Division

On the move, the assault gun battalion attached to an armored division can be used to best advantage if included in the advance guard.

(b) In the Attack with an Infantry Division

The division commander normally attaches assault-gun batteries to the infantry regiments. On receipt of orders placing him under command of an infantry regiment, the battery commander must report in person to the commander of that infantry regiment. Exhaustive discussion between these two (as to enemy situation, preparation of the regiment for the attack, proposed conduct of the attack, main point of the attack, co-operation with divisional artillery, etc.) will provide the basis for the ultimate employment of the assault-gun battery.

It is an error to allot to the battery tasks and targets which can be undertaken by the heavy infantry weapons or the divisional artillery. The battery should rather be employed to engage such nests of resistance as are not known before the beginning of the attack, and which, at the beginning or in the course of the battle, cannot be quickly enough engaged by heavy infantry weapons and artillery. It is the special role of the assault-gun battery to assist the infantry in fighting its way through deep enemy defense zones. Therefore, it must not be committed until the divisional artillery and the heavy infantry weapons can no longer render adequate support.

The attached battery can be employed as follows:

(1) Before the attack begins, it is located so as to be capable of promptly supporting the regiment's main effort; (or)

(2) The battery is held in the rear, and is only committed if, after the attack begins, a clear picture is obtained of the enemy's dispositions.

Under both circumstances the attachment of the battery, and occasionally of individual platoons, to a battalion may be advantageous.

The commander under whose command the battery is placed gives the battery commander his orders. The latter makes clear to his platoon commanders the specific battle tasks, and shows them, as far as possible on the ground, the targets to be engaged. When in action the battery commander, together with his platoon commanders, must at all times be familiar with the hostile situation, and must reconnoiter the ground over which he is to move and attack. The battery will be so disposed by the platoon commanders in the sectors in which it is expected later to operate that, as it approaches the enemy, the battery, under cover, can follow the infantry from sector to sector. How distant an objective can be given, and yet permit the control of fire by the battery and platoon commanders, is dependent on the country, enemy strength, and enemy action. In close country, and when the enemy weapons are well camouflaged, targets cannot be given to the platoons by the battery commander. In these circumstances, fire control falls to the platoon commanders. The platoons must then co-operate constantly with the most advanced infantry platoons; they remain close to the infantry and engage the nearest targets. The question of dividing a platoon arises only if individual guns are allotted to infantry companies or platoons to carry out specific tasks: e.g., for action deep into the enemy's battle position.

In an attack by tanks attached to an infantry division, the assault-artillery battalion engages chiefly enemy antitank weapons. In this case too, the assault-gun battalion is attached to infantry elements. Well before the beginning of the tank attack, the batteries are disposed in positions of observation from which they can readily engage enemy antitank weapons. They follow up the tanks by platoons, and under special conditions—e.g., in unreconnoitered country - by guns, as soon as possible. In a deep attack, co-operation with tanks leading an infantry attack is possible when the hostile islands of resistance have been disposed of.

In the enemy tank counterattack, our own antitank guns first engage the hostile tanks. The assault-gun battalion engages the enemy heavy weapons which are supporting the enemy tank counterattack. Only when the antitank guns prove insufficient, do assault guns engage enemy tanks. In this case the assault guns advance within effective range of the enemy tanks, halt, and destroy them with antitank shells.

(c) In the Attack with an Armored Division

In such an attack, the following tasks can be carried out by the assault gun battalion:

(1) Support of the tank attack by neutralizing enemy antitank weapons; (and/or)

(2) Support of the attack by motorized infantry elements.

According to the situation and the plan of attack, the battalion, complete or in part, is attached to the armored brigade, sometimes with parts attached also to the motorized infantry brigade. Within the armored brigade, further allotment to tank regiments is normally necessary. As a rule, complete batteries are attached.

To support the initial phase of the tank attack, assault-gun batteries can be placed in positions of observation if suitable ground is already in our possession. Otherwise the batteries follow in the attack close behind the first waves of tanks, and as soon as the enemy is engaged, support the tanks by attacking enemy antitank weapons.

As the tank attack progresses, it is most important to put enemy defensive weapons out of action as soon as possible. Close support of the leading tanks is the main essential to the carrying out of these tasks.

The support of the motorized infantry attack is carried out according to the principles for the support of the foot infantry attack.

(d) In the Attack as Divisional Artillery

In the attack of a division, the employment of the assault gun battalion as part of the divisional artillery is exceptional. In this role, the assault-gun batteries must be kept free for their more usual mission at all times, and must enter battle with a full issue of ammunition.

(e) In the Pursuit

In the pursuit, assault-gun batteries should be close to their own infantry in order to break at once any enemy resistance. Very close support of the leading infantry units increases their forward momentum. Temporary allotment of individual platoons—under exceptional circumstances, of individual guns—is possible.

(f) In the Defense

In the defense, the primary task of assault artillery is the support of counterthrusts and counterattacks. The assembly area must be sufficiently far from the friendly battle position to enable the assault-gun units to move speedily to that sector which is threatened with a breakthrough. Allotment and employment are carried out according to the plan of the infantry attack. The point of commitment should be arranged as early as possible with the commanders of the infantry units allocated to the counterthrust or counterattack. In the defense as in the attack, the assault-artillery battalion will only be employed in an antitank role if it must defend itself against a tank attack. (Only 12 percent of the ammunition issue is armor-piercing.) *[15 percent according to the April 1942 document.]* If employed as part of the divisional artillery (which is rare), the battalion will be placed under the division artillery commander.

(g) In the Withdrawal

For the support of infantry in withdrawal, batteries, and even individual platoons or guns, are allotted to infantry units. By virtue of their armor, assault guns are able to engage enemy targets even when the infantry has already withdrawn. To assist disengagement from the enemy, tank attacks carried out with limited objectives can be supported by assault guns. Allotment of assault-gun batteries or platoons to rear parties or rear guards is effective.

d. Supplies

As GHQ troops, the battalion takes with it its complete initial issue of ammunition, fuel, and rations. When it is attached to a division, its further supply is handled by the division. The battalion commander is responsible for the correct supply of the battalion and the individual batteries, especially in the pursuit. Every battery, platoon, and gun commander must constantly have in mind the supply situation of his unit. It is his duty to report his needs in sufficient time and with foresight, and to take the necessary action to replenish depleted supplies of ammunition, fuel, and rations.

26. GERMAN HEAVY TANK

Tactical and Technical Trends, No. 20, March 11th 1943

As reported in the press and as previously indicated in Tactical and Technical Trends (No. 18, p. 6) a German heavy tank has been in action in Tunisia. So far as can be definitely determined, this is the first time the Germans have used a heavy tank in combat. Whether or not it is the Pz.Kw. 6 cannot be definitely stated. At least one heavy tank has been captured, and while complete details are not yet available, there is sufficient reasonably confirmed data to warrant at least a partial tentative description at this time.

The chief features of this tank are the 88-mm gun, 4-inch frontal armor, heavy weight, and lack of spaced armor. The accompanying sketch roughly indicates the appearance of the tank, but should not be accepted as wholly accurate.

The tank has a crew of 5. It is about 20 feet long, 12 feet wide, and 9 1/2 feet high. The gun overhangs the nose by almost 7 feet. It is reported that the weight is 56 tons or, with modifications, as much as 62 tons.

The power unit is a single 12-cylinder engine. A speed of at least 20 mph can be achieved. Two types of track are thought to exist: an operational track 2 feet 4.5 inches wide, and a loading track which is just under 2 feet. The suspension system consists of a front driving sprocket, a small rear idler, and 24 Christie-type wheels on each side giving it an appearance similar to the familiar German half-track suspension system. There are 8 axles.

There is no armor skirting for protection of the suspension. The armor plating is as follows:

- Lower nose plate - 62 mm (2.4 in), 60° inwards
- Upper nose plate - 102 mm (4 in), 20° inwards
- Front plate - 62 mm (2.4 in), 80° outwards
- Driver plate - 102 mm (4 in), 10° outwards
- Turret sides and rear - 82 mm (3.2 in), vertical

- Lower sides (behind bogies) - 62 mm (2.4 in), vertical
- Upper sides - 82 mm (3.2 in), vertical
- Rear - 82 mm (3.2 in), 20° inwards
- Floor - 26 mm (1 in)
- Top - 26 mm (1 in)

The turret front and mantlet range in thickness between a minimum of 97 mm (3.8 in) to a (possible) maximum of 200 mm (7.9 in). It appears that the armor is not face-hardened.

The armament of the tank consists of an 88-mm gun and two 7.92-mm (.315-in) machine guns. The 88-mm has a double-baffle muzzle brake and fires the same fixed ammunition as the usual 88-mm AA/AT gun. As already indicated, the gun overhangs the nose of the tank by almost 7 feet. The turret rotates through 360 degrees and is probably power-operated. Three smoke-generator dischargers are located on each side of the turret.

Comment: From the above characteristics, it is apparent that the Pz.Kw. 6 is designed to be larger and more powerful than the Pz.Kw. 4. As far as known, a Pz.Kw. 5 tank has not been used in combat. The noteworthy differences between the Pz.Kw. 4 and Pz.Kw. 6 are as follows:

Armor	Pz.Kw. 4	Pz.Kw. 6
Minimum	20 mm	26 mm
Maximum	50 to 80 mm*	102 mm**
Principal Armament	75-mm (long-barrelled gun)	88-mm (AA/AT gun)

*Attained by attaching extra armor plate to protect critical points on the tank.
**Basic armor plate. The turret front and mantlet may possibly be 200 mm thick.

A 360-degree rotating turret is used in both the Pz.Kw. 6 and Pz.Kw. 4.

The appearance of the Pz.Kw. 6 indicates that the Germans continue to see the need for a fully armored vehicle equipped with a weapon capable of dealing with hostile tanks as well as with other targets that might hold up the advance of attacking elements.

This tank is undoubtedly an effective weapon, but not necessarily formidable. In the first place, a vehicle weighing from 56 to 62 tons presents many difficult logistical problems. Also, it is reported that one heavy tank was destroyed by a British six-pounder (57-mm) antitank gun at a range of about 500 yards; out of 20 rounds fired, 5 penetrated the tank, 1 piercing the side of the turret and coming out the other side, and another penetrating an upper side plate at an angle of impact of about 15 degrees.

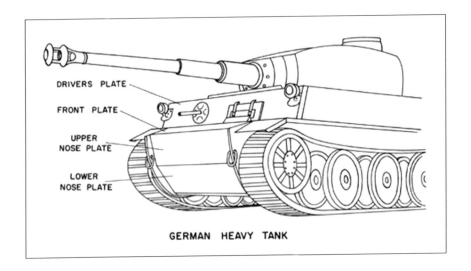

DRIVERS PLATE

FRONT PLATE

UPPER
NOSE PLATE

LOWER
NOSE PLATE

GERMAN HEAVY TANK

27. FURTHER INFORMATION ABOUT GERMAN TANKS

Intelligence Bulletin, September 1943

1. ARMOR ARRANGEMENT

The sketches on the next three pages show the armor arrangement and armor thicknesses of the Pz. Kw. 3, Pz. Kw. 4, and Pz. Kw. 6. A question mark following a figure indicates that definite information regarding the thickness of a certain plate is not yet available. Two figures enclosed in parentheses indicate the presence of two plates, which are separated to form "spaced armor"; this arrangement occurs only twice, and only in the case of the Pz. Kw. 3.

Figure 1
[This figure caption was corrected in a footnote of a later issue of Intelligence Bulletin to: "Pz. Kw. 3 with 50-mm gun (Kw. K. 39)".]

2. SUBMERSIBLE TANKS

The delays and difficulties that the Germans have encountered in transporting tanks across the rivers of Eastern Europe have increased

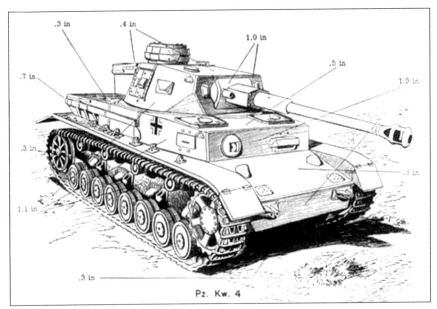

Figure 2

the enemy's interest in all possible devices which might enable standard Pz. Kw. to cross streams and rivers under their own power.

By the summer of 1941, the weight of the Pz. Kw. 3 had already been increased by additional armor, and it must have been clear to the Germans that future developments in armor and armament would necessarily involve still further increases in the weight of this tank. While the trend toward increased weight was a disadvantage in many ways, it was definitely helpful in overcoming one of the biggest difficulties that the Germans had previously encountered in adapting standard tanks for submersion—namely, the difficulty of getting enough track adhesion.

It therefore is not surprising that the Germans, in the early stages of their campaign in Russia, were actively experimenting with standard Pz. Kw. 3's modified for submersion. It is reported that these experiments met with a certain amount of success, and that the modified tanks made underwater river crossings under combat conditions. The measures employed are said to have included the sealing of all joints and openings in the tank with rubber and the introduction of a flexible air pipe, the free end of which was attached to a float. The supply of air for the crew, as well as for the engine, was provided by this flexible pipe, which permitted submersion to a maximum depth of 16 feet. It took trained crews 24 hours to prepare the tanks for submersion.

In April 1943, a Pz. Kw. 3 (Model M) examined in North Africa was found to have been permanently modified for immersion, if not for submersion. Although reports on this tank did not mention a flexible pipe with float, such a pipe may have existed and have been destroyed by fire. The air louvres for the engine were provided with cover plates having rubber sealing strips round their edges. These cover plates, which were normally held open by strong springs, could be locked in the closed position by hooks before submersion. After submersion, the springs could be released by controls inside the tank. When the tank submerged, air for the carburetor and cooling fans was apparently drawn from the fighting compartment. Therefore, if a flexible pipe was used with this tank, no doubt its purpose was to supply "replacement" air to the fighting compartment. The two exhaust pipes led to a single silencer mounted high on the tail plate, with its outlet at the top. This outlet was fitted with a spring-controlled, one-way valve, which could be kept in the fully open

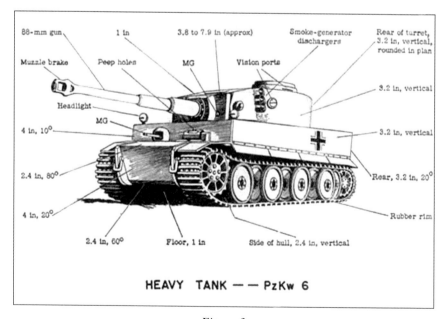

Figure 3

position during normal operation on land.

More recently, documents and reports from Russia have shown that the standard Pz. Kw. 6 (Tiger) is equipped for submersion to depths of as much as 16 feet. In this tank there is provision for hermetic sealing of all joints and openings. The doors and covers are provided with suitable rubber seals. The radiators are separated from the engine by a watertight partition so that, when the tank is submerged, they can be cooled by water from outside the tank, after the cooling fans have been switched off. In this case carburetor air is drawn through a flexible pipe, the free end of which is supported by a float, but there appears to be no additional supply of air for the crew. A small bilge pump is also fitted to dispose of any water which may leak into the hull.

It is clear that the Pz. Kw. 6 requires only a slight amount of preparation by its crew before submersion, and that its design must have been influenced by the requirement that it quickly be made submersible. It is quite possible that the Pz. Kw. 3 could be submerged to a depth of more than 16 feet if it were fitted with a longer air pipe. Although the Pz. Kw. 6 is not much larger than the Pz. Kw. 3, it is nearly three times as heavy, and track adhesion is therefore not likely to be a serious problem.

28. TANK RUSE TO DECEIVE ARTILLERY

Intelligence Bulletin, September 1943

U.S. artillerymen—and forward observers, in particular—will be interested in a ruse which was employed by a German tank unit in Tunisia. This tank force was located by a U.S. observer, who immediately prepared fire data to rout the enemy. Fire promptly got under way. At the second volley, the Germans put into operation a plan designed to confuse our artillerymen:

The Germans calculated the time of flight of the projectiles, and then listened for the report of the third volley. When it came, they shrewdly took the time element into account and fired their own tank pieces to conform with the strike of our own artillery fire. The Germans directed their fire first to one of their flanks and then to the other, at various ranges. Since our own artillery fire fell simultaneously in the same general area, our forward observer was unable to distinguish our fire from the enemy's and therefore could not register.

This continued for several minutes, with the artillery observer frantically trying to figure out the correct deflection and range. Then, by means of close observation, he discovered the technique that the Germans were using, and soon had them on the run.

As a U.S. soldier who took part in this action expresses it, "There's one thing we've always got to remember: in fighting the Germans, we're up against a cunning, imaginative enemy!"

29. GERMAN HEAVY TANK - PZKW 6

Tactical and Technical Trends, No. 24, May 6th 1943

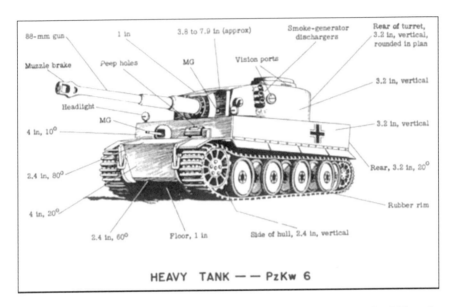

This tank has already been described in Tactical and Technical Trends (No. 20, p. 7). The accompanying sketch of the tank is based on photographs of a PzKw 6 knocked out on the Tunisian front.

The suspension system, which has only very briefly been described in Tactical and Technical Trends, is shown in the sketch below. The track is made of metal. To the far right in the sketch is the front-drive sprocket and to the far left, the rear Idler. There are no return rollers since the track rides on top of the Christie-type wheels, which are rubber rimmed. It will be noted that there are eight axles, each with three wheels to a side, or each with one single and one double wheel to a side. There are thus 24 wheels, or 8 single wheels and 8 double wheels, on each side of the tank. The system of overlapping is similar to the suspension system used on German half-tracks.

The tank is provided with two tracks, a wide one (2 ft, 4.5 in) and a narrow one (just under 2 ft). The wide track is the one used in battle, the narrow being for administrative marches and where maneuverability and economy of operation take precedence over ground pressure. The dotted line in the sketch of the suspension system indicates the outer edge of the narrow track. When the narrow track is used, the eight wheels outside the dotted line can be removed.

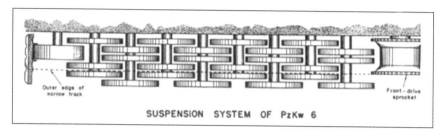

Outer edge of narrow track

Front-drive sprocket

SUSPENSION SYSTEM OF PzKw 6

30. INCREASED PROTECTION ON PZKW 3 AND 4

Tactical and Technical Trends, No. 25, May 20th 1943

The history of the changes in the light medium PzKw 3 and 4 demonstrates how fortunate the Germans were in having a basic tank design that could be improved as battle experience indicated, for a basic design can be improved and still remain familiar to the users. Furthermore, the problems of maintenance and supply of parts are greatly reduced—and these problems are a major factor in keeping tanks ready for operational use.

a. The PzKw 3

(1) General

The Germans seem to be making a gradual increase in thickness of armor-plate as the guns used against it increase in hitting power and range. The PzKw 3 medium tank is illustrative of this trend in tank armor and design, and affords a remarkable example of what can be done to improve the armor protection and fighting efficiency of a tank without changing its basic design. The key of this basic design is the welded main structure which allows heavier plates to be used when desired. Also, operating components of the tank are not hung on the plates, likely to be changed to thicker ones.

(2) Pre-War

The early model PzKw 3 (produced in 1936-38) had basic armor of .59-inch homogeneous plate. At this time there were only 5 bogie wheels on a side instead of the present 6. There is a gap in the formation until 1939, when the tank appeared with 1.18-inch face-hardened armor on the turret and front. This model had 6 bogie wheels on the side. The side armor which forms a great part of the chassis was of softer, machineable-quality plate, due both to necessities of manufacture and to the undesirable weakening effect on hardened plate of the necessary suspension and bracket holes. The model also had improved aperture protection in the form of an external moving mantlet, additional armor around the machine-gun port, and an improved double-flap driver's visor. It appears that these features were added with the modification of but 2 plates on the tank.

(3) 1941 Changes

In 1941, as more powerful guns were being used against tanks, 1.20 inches of additional armor plate was bolted against the plates on the front of the superstructure and on the upper and lower nose-plates. The 1.18-in. basic plates were face-hardened to a Brinell hardness of 600 to 800 and 1.20-in additional plates were the same. About a year later, in January 1942, the tank appeared with a basic armor of 1.96 inches on the front and back, the side-armor thickness remaining unchanged at 1.20 inches. This armor was face-hardened and performed well against monobloc shot, but once the face-hardening was pierced, the shell fragments penetrated the remainder with ease.

(4) 1942

Therefore, in June 1942, a .79-inch additional plate was bolted on the gun mantlet and front superstructure as a means to defeat a shot with a piercing cap. Between this plate and the basic armor was an air gap or space, varying from 4 to 8 inches. The plate conformed roughly to the shape of the section covered. The spaced armor seems to have been a field expedient, resulting undoubtedly from the demonstrated fact that the spare section of track carried on the front of German tanks gave additional protection. This method of adding armor was officially recognized, as later models had brackets fitted for installing spaced armor when desirable.

b. PzKw 4

(1) Early Models

The PzKw 4, a slightly heavier tank than the 3, has passed through much the same line of development. Little is known about the models A, B, and C of this tank, but Model D was in use during the greater part of the period 1940-43. Specimens of armor cut from Model D have been examined. Of these, only the front plate of the hull appears to be face-hardened; this plate is carburized. All of the plates were high-quality, chromium-molybdenum steel, apparently made by the electric-furnace process.

The first increase in the armor of this tank was reported in 1941, when it was observed that additional plates had been bolted over the basic front and side armor. The additional plates on the front were 1.18 inches thick, making a total of 2.36 inches, and those on the sides were .79 inches thick, making a total of 1.57 inches. In its early stages, this addition was probably only an improvised measure for increasing the armor protection of existing PzKw 4 models in which the thickest armor was only 1.18 inches.

(2) Model E

In Model E, which had 1.96 inches of single-thickness nose plate, the fitting of additional armor on the front of the superstructure and on the sides of the fighting compartment was continued. Although the arrangement of the additional side armor on this model appears to have been standardized, that on the front superstructure was by no means uniform.

Three PzKw 4 tanks have recently been examined. In each case, extra armor had been fitted to the vertical front plate carrying the hull machine gun and driver's visor. It had also been added to the sides of the fighting compartment both above and below the track level. The extra protection above the track level extended from the front vertical plate to the end of the engine-compartment bulkhead. It was thus 110 inches long and 15 inches deep. The pieces below the track level were shaped in such a way as to clear the suspension brackets. They were 90 inches long and 30 inches deep. All this extra side protection was .97 inch in thickness.

The vertical front plate was reinforced in three different ways. On one tank, two plates were used; one over the plate carrying the hull machine gun, this additional plate being cut away to suit the gun mounting, and the other plate over the driver's front plate, cut to shape to clear his visor. On the second tank, the arrangement around the hull gun was the same, but the extra protection around the driver's visor consisted of two rectangular plates, one on each side of the visor, there being no extra plate immediately above the visor. On the third tank, the only additional front armor was the plate around the hull machine gun. No additions had been made to the driver's front plate. In all cases, the extra frontal plating was 1.18 inches thick; the nose plate was unreinforced, but it was 1.97 inches thick, and the glacis plate was .97 inch thick. The final drive casings of PzKw 4 tanks of this period were also sometimes reinforced by .79-inch protecting rings. The additional plates on the front were face-hardened.

It is probable that the reinforced armor on the front superstructure of this model will compare closely with that on the corresponding parts of the PzKw 3 of 1941 and that the 1.96-inch nose plates will not differ substantially from those on the more recent PzKw 3's of June 1942, known as "Model J."

The reinforced (.79 inch plus .79 inch) side armor has, however, no counterpart in any PzKw 3 model. The additional plates are of homogeneous quality and have a Brinell hardness of about 370 on the front surface.

(3) Model F

Towards the end of 1941 the Germans introduced a PzKw 4, Model F, having 1.96-inch frontal armor (gun mantlet, front superstructure and hull nose-plates) and 1.18-inch side armor. In this and many other respects, the Model F conforms more closely than its predecessors to the corresponding model of the PzKw 3 (in this case PzKw 3 Model J). So far, the armor of the PzKw 4 Model F has not been examined to ascertain its chemical and ballistic properties, but there is a strong probability that these do not differ greatly from those of the PzKw 3, Model J.

(4) Model G

This model which mounts the long 75-mm gun, Kw.K 40, was first encountered in June 1942. It is reported from the Middle East that its armor is the same as that of Model F; namely 1.96 inches on the front, and 30 mm (1.18 inches) on the sides.

31. ENEMY SELF-PROPELLED GUNS - A SUMMARY OF KNOWN EQUIPMENT

Tactical and Technical Trends, No. 25, May 20th 1943

a. General

Self-propelled guns represent one of the technical advances made in ordnance during this war. The following account, from British sources, of German, Italian, and Japanese equipment shows the considerable interest which this development has aroused. Several descriptions and sketches of these guns have already been published in earlier issues of Tactical and Technical Trends.

With reference to German self-propelled guns the following general points are worthy of note:

There are no known German self-propelled heavy antiaircraft guns;

With regard to antitank guns, while there have been many local improvisations, the present German tendency is to provide self-propelled mounts for the heavier antitank weapons only;

Fig. I

In every case standard guns and standard chassis, whether semi- or full-tracked, are used;

All self-propelled guns are provided with AP and HE ammunition, and can thus effectively engage both "soft" and armored targets.

b. German AA/AT Guns

(1) 20-mm AA AT Gun

Although primarily an antiaircraft gun, this piece can also be used against tanks. Mounted on a 1-ton half-track (see figure 1) with a gasoline engine, it usually tows a single-axle ammunition trailer. The armament is a long, thin-barreled, 20-mm, high-velocity gun. The weight in action is 4.5 tons; the length, 15 ft. 7 in., the width, 7 ft. 1 in. and the height, 6 ft. 7 in. On roads, the radius of action is about 137 miles; cross country, about 93. The crew is seven men.

There are two versions of the gun itself, namely the 20-mm Flak 30 and the 20-mm Flak 38. The gun, mounted in front, may or may not be shielded. It fires 20-mm, .260-pound, high-explosive shells at a high muzzle velocity of 2,950 f/s, the .327-pound AP shell at 2,625 f/s, and the .223-pound AP 40 shot at 3,270 f/s. The firing rate is 120 rpm. The horizontal range is 5,320 yards. The mount gives an all-around traverse and an elevation varying from minus 12 degrees to plus 90. At 400 yards, the AP shell will pierce .98 inch of homogenous armor at an impact angle of 30 degrees, and 1.50 inches at normal. At 400 yards' range, the AP 40 shot will pierce 1.46 inches at 30 degrees, and 1.69 inches at normal.

(2) 20-mm Four-Barreled AA/AT Gun

This is a Vierling (quadruple) gun on an 8-ton half-track (see Tactical and Technical Trends, No. 4, p. 4) 22 ft. 6 in. long by 7 ft. 11 in. wide and 10 ft. 10 in. high, weighing, ready for action, 11.5 tons. The gasoline engine develops 140 brake horse power, giving a radius of action on the road of 155 miles, and about 62 cross country. The crew is probably eight. The armament is "a quadruple 20-mm Flak 38, with an all-around traverse and an elevation stated as from "minus 10 to plus 100" (apparently 10 degrees past vertical—which seems odd, but may be useful when firing at planes passing directly

FIG. 2

overhead). The range, penetration, and ammunition are substantially the same as for the Flak 30 and 38 previously noted.

(3) 37-mm AA/AT Gun

While like the 20-mm primarily an antiaircraft gun, this 37-mm gun can be used for horizontal fire. It may be identified by the long, slender barrel with a conical muzzle brake (see figure 2), and it usually tows an ammunition trailer. The mount is a 5-ton, half-tracked vehicle, with a 130-HP gasoline motor giving a 156-mile radius on the road, and about 62 miles cross country (which seems rather small). The length and breadth are 20 ft. 7 in. by 7 ft. 6 in.; the height is 9 ft. 2 in. The crew is eight men.

Like the 20-mm, the 37-mm Flak 36 is a high-velocity gun, delivering an HE shell at 2,690 f/s at the muzzle. The horizontal range is slightly over 7,000 yards, and the rate of fire, 60 rpm. There is all-around traverse, and an elevation of from minus 5 to plus 85 degrees.

(4) 50-mm Self-Propelled AA/AT Gun

This weapon, the 5-cm Flak 41, is known to exist, but details are lacking. Presumably, it may be a development of the standard 50-mm antitank gun (5-cm Pak 38) described in Tactical and Technical Trends, No. 15, p. 38, which gives a reported muzzle velocity of 3,940 f/s to an AP shot of 2.025 pounds, and 2,740 f/s to a 4 lb. 9 oz. AP tracer shell.

(5) 88-mm Self-Propelled Multi-Purpose Gun

A self-propelled version of the "88," the 8.8-cm Flak 36 Sfl, is known to exist. At one time the gun was said to be mounted on a 12-ton half-track, but this mounting is believed to have been unsatisfactory. Various other mounts have been reported, the most likely of which is the PzKw 4 (medium tank) chassis. In this case, the gun probably has a limited traverse and cannot deliver antiaircraft fire. It fires a 20-pound HE shell, or a 21-pound AP, with an armor-piercing cap surmounted by a "wind splitter" ballistic cap. At 500 yards the projectile will penetrate 4.33 inches of armor at a 30-degree angle, and 5.07 inches at normal. When the range is lengthened to 1,000 yards, penetration falls to 3.30 and 3.93 inches, respectively. The maximum horizontal range is 16,200 yards, but the sight is graduated to 10,340 yards only. The practical rate of fire is from 15 to 20 rpm. The number in the crew is not stated.

c. German Self-Propelled Antitank Guns
(1) 28-mm AT Gun, Model 41

It may be that this gun is a local improvisation. Firing forward, it is mounted on a light half-track, with a coffin-shaped, armored body.

The small weapon may be identified by its prominent muzzle brake and flat, double shield. The chassis is that of a 1-ton half-tracked vehicle. The battle weight is about 6 tons. The dimensions are 15 ft. 6 in. by 6 ft. by 7 ft.; the motor is a 100-hp gasoline engine. Cross country, the radius of action is about 75 miles; on the road, 120. Varying from about .39 inch on the front, the light armor is .32 inch elsewhere. The crew is believed to number five.

The ultra-modern, high-velocity gun is the 2.8-cm (1.1 in) Pz.B. 41. It is choke-bored from 28 mm at the breech to 20 (.79 in) at the muzzle, and has a muzzle velocity of 4,580 f/s. At 100 yards it will drive a .287-pound shot through 2.72 inches of armor at 30 degrees, and through 3.31 inches at normal angle. At 100 yards the penetrations are 2.09 and 2.56 inches, respectively. The traverse is 90 degrees, the elevation from minus 5 to plus 45.

(2) 37-mm AT Gun

Like the 28-mm, this gun may be a local improvisation. The obsolete 37-mm antitank gun, with or without a shield, fires towards the front and is mounted on a 3-ton armored half-track; weight in action is 8.4 tons (see figure 3). The dimensions are: length 18 ft. 8 in., width 6 ft. 10 in., height about 7 ft. 6 in. The gasoline motor develops 100 hp. On the road, the radius is 187 miles, and 81 across country. In front, the armor is from .39 inch to .59 inch in thickness,

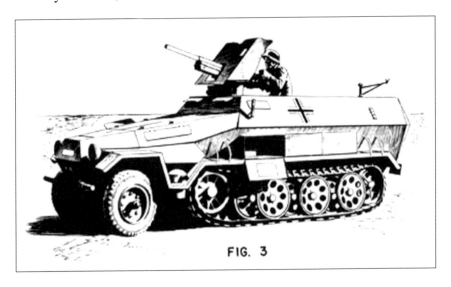

FIG. 3

and on the sides, .32 inch. The crew numbers three.

This gun has a muzzle velocity of 2,500 f/s for the 1.68-pound AP shell and 3,380 (estimated) for the .786-pound AP 40. The HE weighs 1.38 pounds. At 200 yards, the AP shell will penetrate 1.65 inches at 30 degrees and 2.20 inches at normal angle; at 600 yards, 1.34 and 1.81 inches, respectively. The AP 40 at 100 yards pierces 2.68 inches at 30 degrees and 3.11 inches, normal; but with the light AP 40 shot, at 400 yards, the penetration falls to 1.93 and 2.28 inches. The effective range is 600 yards. The maximum traverse is 60 degrees, and the elevation varies from minus 8 to plus 25 degrees.

(3) 47-mm AT Gun

This piece of equipment is the Czech antitank gun mounted in a three-sided shield on the turretless chassis of the PzKw 1 Model B tank. It may be recognized by the five bogie wheels (of which the rear four are partially obscured by a girder), a front sprocket, a rear idler, and four return rollers. The gun-shield is open at the back and top. The gun is fitted with a muzzle brake, and the recuperator is above the barrel. The weight is 7.5 tons; the dimensions 13 ft. 7 in., 6 ft. 7 in., and 7 ft. A 100-hp gasoline engine will drive the vehicle on a radius of action of 70 miles cross country and 90 on the road. The crew is three.

The Skoda gun has a 30-degree traverse with an elevation of from minus 8 degrees to plus 12. The AP tracer shell, 3.68 pounds, has a velocity of 2,540 f/s, penetrating at 300 yards 2.32 inches of armor at 30 degrees, and 2.99 inches at normal angle. At 1,000 yards the respective penetrations are 1.85 and 2.44 inches. An HE shell of 5.07 pounds and an AP 40 shot of 1.81 pounds are used. The effective range is not stated, but is apparently 1,000 yards. About 74 rounds are carried.

(4) 50-mm AT Gun

The only evidence of this equipment is a photograph, which showed a long-barreled gun in a fixed, square turret on an armored half-tracked vehicle of unconventional design. There is a large muzzle brake at the end of the gun, which is believed to be the standard 50-mm Pak 38.

(5) 75-mm AT Gun, on a PzKw 38(t) Chassis

This equipment consists of the 75-mm (2.95-in) antitank gun (Pak 40) mounted on the turretless chassis of the light Czech PzKw 38(t). The suspension consists of four large Christie-type bogie wheels, two return rollers (mounted above the space between bogie wheels 1 and 2, and 2 and 3, respectively), a front sprocket, and a rear idler. In action, the weight is 10 tons. The dimensions are 15 ft. 3 in. by 7 ft. by 7 ft. 2 in. A 125-hp gasoline motor gives a radius of 143 miles on the road, 103 cross country. A plate of .98-inch armor with, possibly, an additional plate of the same thickness riveted on, protects the front. The sides are 1.18 inches toward the front, and .59 inch toward the rear of the sides and the back of the hull. The crew is probably four.

The gun is a 75-mm antitank piece, thought to have a performance similar to the 75-mm long-barreled tank gun mounted in the latest PzKw 4's. This latter gun has the moderate velocity of 2,400 f/s, giving a penetration (presumably with a 15-pound, capped AP projectile) of 3.5 inches at 500 yards at a 30-degree angle, and 4.25 inches at normal. At 2,000 yards, the shell pierces 2.44 and 3.03 inches. There is an AP 40 shot supplied for this gun, and a 12.5-pound HE shell.

(6) 75-mm AT Gun on a PzKw 2 Chassis

This 10-ton assembly may be recognized by the long-barreled gun with the muzzle brake, as in the previous description, but the PzKw 2 chassis has either five or six large bogie wheels. Its length is 15 ft. 2 in., width, 1 ft. 4 in., and height 16 ft. 6 in. With a 140-hp gasoline engine, the radius on the road is 118 miles, and cross country 78 miles. In front, the armor varies from .59 inch to 1.79 inch, with .59 inch on the back and sides. The crew is probably four. The gun is the same one described in the previous paragraph.

(7) 76.2-mm (3-in) AT Gun on a 5-Ton Half-Track

Possibly another local improvisation, this piece of equipment consists of a Russian 76.2-mm gun mounted on the chassis of a 5-ton half-track in a high, square, box-like riveted structure of .20-inch armor, Open at the top (see figure 4). The gun may be employed both in field artillery and antitank roles.

FIG. 4

The weight is about 10 tons. The mount is 19 ft. 9 in. long, 7 ft. 3 in. wide, and 10 ft. high. The motor is a 130-hp gasoline engine, giving the weapon a radius of action of 160 miles on roads and 70 across country, carrying a crew of probably six.

The 76.2-mm Russian field gun Model 36 (7.62-cm Pak 36 (r)) with a long, thin barrel throws a 14.8-pound capped armor-piercing shell at the relatively low velocity of 2,200 f/s, a 14-pound HE at 2,340 f/s, and an AP 40 shot of 9.25 pounds weight at 2,800 f/s. The range is not stated, but the firing charts include ranges up to 2,000 yards, at which range it is claimed that the AP shell will drive through 2.08 inches of armor with a 30-degree slope, and 2.52 inches, vertical. At 500 yards, the penetration is reported to be 3.11 and 3.70 inches, respectively. The awkward-appearing mount gives an unexpectedly large traverse of 60 degrees, with an elevation varying from minus 5 to plus 45 degrees. (The gun mount is capable of giving 75 degrees of elevation, but the shield fouls the front tarpaulin rail at 45 degrees.) Sixty-four rounds are carried, approximately half HE and half AP.

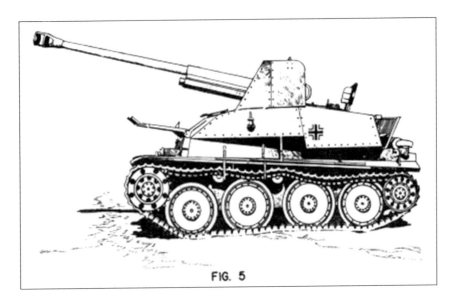

FIG. 5

(8) 76.2-mm Gun on Tank Chassis

This is the 76.2-mm Russian gun just discussed, mounted on the light Czech PzKw 38(t) chassis with 4 bogies as described in Tactical And Technical Trends, No. 21, p. 6 (see figure 5); it is also mounted on the PzKw 2 chassis which has 5 bogie wheels. Both chassis are rather light for so large a gun. It seems unlikely that either the traverse or elevation on these tank chassis is as great as on the 5-ton half-track.

d. German Self-Propelled Assault Guns

(1) 75-mm Assault Gun

A low silhouette, a well-armored body, and a short gun firing forward characterize this assault gun. (See Tactical and Technical Trends, No. 7, p. 9.) The mount is the chassis of the PzKw 3. The suspension consists of six small bogies or each side with three return rollers, a front sprocket, and a rear idler. The vehicle with its weapon is heavy—nearly 20 tons. It is 17 ft. 9 in. long and 9 ft. 7 in. wide, but only 6 ft. 5 in. high. A radius of 102 miles by road and 59 cross country is attained with a 300-hp gasoline motor. The crew is four. Probably, this model is no longer in production.

With its casemate mount, the short-barreled 75-mm gun has a traverse of only 20 degrees, and an elevation varying from minus 5 to plus 20. For HE shell, the gun is sighted to 6,550 yards; for AP, only 1,640. At 500 yards, the penetration is 1.81 inches in 30-degree sloping armor, and 2.16 inches in vertical; at 1,200, it drops to 1.57 and 1.89 inches. The HE shell weighs 12.6 pounds; the AP shell, with cap and ballistic cap, 14.81. There is an AP hollow charge of unstated weight, as well as a 13.56-pound smoke shell. In the bins of the carrier, 44 rounds are carried, and about 40 more may be stacked on the floor. A dozen stick grenades (potato mashers) may also be carried clipped on a rack.

(2) 75-mm Medium-Length Assault Gun

This machine is essentially similar to the foregoing, except that a gun 30 calibers long mounted in a large box-like casing has replaced the stubby piece in the earlier model.

(3) 75-mm Long Assault Gun

The third assault gun model is a long-barreled "75" with a prominent muzzle brake. It, too, is mounted on the PzKw 3 chassis (see figure 6). The velocity has been increased to 2,400 f/s, with a resulting increased penetration at 500 yards of 3.5 inches of sloping armor and 4.25 inches of vertical; at 2,000, the penetration is still formidable—2.44 and 3.03 inches. It is thought that this gun is primarily a tank-destroyer weapon.

Fig. 6

(4) 75-mm Gun Mounted on a 3-Ton Half-Track

Probably another local improvisation, this weapon is mounted on an armored half-track. The mounting is the same as that used for the 37-mm anti-tank gun, the details of which are given in c (2) above. (If the 76.2 Russian gun is a little heavy for a PzKw 2 mount, a 3-ton half-track would seem extremely light for a 75-mm piece.)

(5) 150-mm Infantry Howitzer on PzKw 1 Chassis

Probably retaining its original wheels and trail, this medium howitzer is mounted on the semiobsolete PzKw 1-B chassis. This chassis has five bogies (of which the rear four are partially obscured by a girder), four return rollers, a front sprocket, and a rear idler. Above the chassis floor is a high, three-sided gun shield, open on the top and back. The weight is about 9 tons. In length, it is 13 ft. 7 in.; in width, 6 ft. 7 in.; and the height is 11 ft. A radius of 95 miles on the road and 70 miles cross country is given by a 100-hp gasoline engine. Front and sides are protected by .59-inch armor, and back by .28 inches, and the gun shield is thought to be 'only about .39 inch. Four men make up the crew.

The piece is the normal 150-mm heavy infantry howitzer (15-cm s.I.G.33) with a muzzle velocity of 790 f/s and a range of 5,125 yards. The recuperator is underneath, and extends almost to the end of, the short barrel. On the field mounting, the traverse is 11 degrees, and the elevation from 0 to 73 degrees. Ammunition weights are 83.6 pounds for the HE shell, and 84.7 for the smoke.

(6) 150-mm Infantry Howitzer on PzKw 2 Chassis

A close-support piece of great power has been made by mounting a 150-mm howitzer low behind a three-sided shield on what is possibly a redesigned PzKw 2 chassis. (See Tactical and Technical Trends, No. 22, p. 13, and No. 13, p. 6.) In place of the usual five large bogie wheels, there are six (see figure 7), suggesting that the normal PzKw 2 chassis has been lengthened, or a new chassis designed. There are four return rollers, a front sprocket, and a rear idler. The weight is about 11 tons. The length is about 18 ft.; the width is 7 ft. 4 in.; and the height has been kept down to 5 ft. 6 in.—a remarkably low silhouette. A 140-hp motor gives a radius of action

FIG. 7

of 118 miles on the road and 78 miles across country. The frontal armor consists of two plates, .59 and .79 inch thick. Sides, back, and shield have .59 inch, and the superstructure .39 inch. The crew is probably four. As in the previously described weapon, the gun is a short heavy infantry howitzer, with the recuperator almost as long as the barrel.

e. German Self-Propelled Medium Artillery

(1) 105-mm Gun

Nothing is known of the mount except that it is armored. The gun is thought to be the standard 10-cm K 18 of which the following are some of the particulars: muzzle velocity 2,660 f/s; maximum effective antitank range, 2,060 yards; penetration with 34.6-pound armor-piercing shell at 500 yards, 30 degrees slope, 5.49 inches, and vertical, 6.46 inches; penetrations at 2,000 yards, 4.39 and 5.22 inches. A capped, AP shell and a 33.5-pound HE shell are reported.

(2) 105-mm Gun-Howitzer

Nothing is known of the mount, but the gun performances are believed to be as follows: muzzle velocity (super-charge), 1,540 f/s; range, 11,640 yards. Shell weights vary between 31.25 pounds for the AP tracer to 35.9 pounds for the hollow-charge.

(3) 128-mm Gun

Both this gun and the 105 were probably produced to deal with the heaviest Russian tanks. No details are available as to the gun or the mount.

(4) 150-mm Howitzer on French 38L Mount

Attention is called to the account in Tactical and Technical Trends, No. 12, p. 15 of this 150-mm howitzer mounted on the 6-bogie chassis of the French tracteur blindé 38L (see figure 8). The hull is divided into 3 compartments: the driving compartment in the front, the engine in the center, and a deep, well-protected cockpit for the gun crew in the rear. The assembly is light (7 1/2 tons). It is 14 ft. long and 5 ft. 2 in. wide, with a 70-hp engine giving a speed of 22 mph. The radius of action is not stated. Armor protection is from .37 to .47 inch in front, .35 inch on sides and rear, and .24 inch on the superstructure. The fixed gun housing, mounted in the floor of the chassis, is of rather thin plate. Traverse is limited to about 4 degrees, and a rear spade is provided to take up recoil stresses. The crew is four.

While the 150-mm assault guns, previously described, are 150-mm infantry howitzers firing an 86-pound shell, this medium howitzer has a longer barrel, which gives a muzzle velocity of 1,250

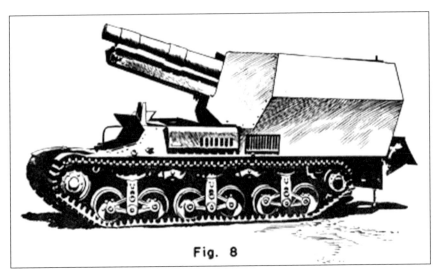

Fig. 8

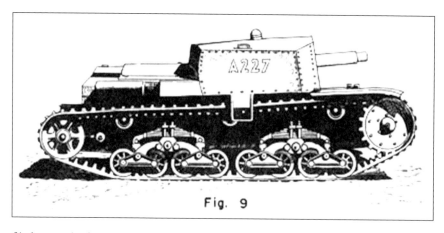

Fig. 9

f/s instead of 790 to a shell of 92.4 pounds weight. The range is 9,300 yards as against 5,125. HE shells, and anticoncrete and smoke shells, are provided. It is notable that in this case a self-propelled gun firing a 92-pound shell to so great a range has been developed on a weight limit of 7.5 tons.

f. Italian Self-Propelled Guns
(1) 75/18 Gun-Howitzer

This seemingly effective, self-propelled equipment is the chassis of the M13, mounting a 75/18 gun-howitzer (see figure 9). The turret and part of the superstructure of the tank are removed, and a new vertical front plate is fitted, as well as new side plates without the hull entrance-doors. The fighting compartment is roofed with .39-inch plate. Ready for action, the gun weighs about 11 tons. It is 16 ft. 2 in. long, 7 ft. 3 in. wide, and only 5 ft. 10 in. high, presenting a rather squat appearance. The unusual engine is a 105-hp Gasolio, burning a mixture of gasoline and fuel oil. On the roads, the radius is about 120 miles. The cross-country radius is not stated. The armor is substantial: 1.69 inches on the gun mantlet, and two plates, 1.46 and .91 inches, forming the front vertical plate. Sides and tail plates are .98 inch. The crew is three.

The gun has a traverse of 45 degrees and an elevation of from 15 degrees minus to 25 degrees plus. It is an 18 caliber weapon with a maximum range of 8,350 yards. The ammunition consists of 13.9-pound HE shell, 14.1-pound AP and a 14.5-pound shrapnel. Storage for only 29 rounds is provided, but many more will certainly be carried.

(2) The 75/27 Gun, Truck-Mounted

It has been reported that there is in service a somewhat clumsy self-propelled mount comprising a 75/27 gun on the back of an unarmored "S.P.A." truck. The standard small shield is retained and a second small shield mounted in front of it; the trail legs are shortened and clamped to the chassis. The gun fires forward over the hood of the truck.

The gun is rather better than the 75/18, with a muzzle velocity of 1,675 f/s. The elevation is from minus 15 to plus 65 degrees; the traverse is practically 60 degrees. In addition to the HE, shrapnel, and AP shell already noted, the gun fires a 13.79-pound streamlined HE, a 15.9-pound case-shot,* and a hollow-charge shell.

(3) 75/27 Antiaircraft Gun, Truck-Mounted

This is an obsolete 75/27 Krupp antiaircraft gun mounted on a Ceirano 50 C.M.A. 53-hp truck, or a Fiat 18 BL 40-hp truck. Both are four wheeled. The Ceirano truck has a radius of 150 miles on the road; the Fiat, 112. The gun has a muzzle velocity of only 1,675 f/s, with a horizontal range of 6,600 yards and vertical range of 15,200 feet. The elevation is 70 degrees, the traverse 160. A 14.5-pound, time-fuzed, HE shell is fired.

(4) 90/53 AA/AT Gun, Truck-Mounted

This is a 90/53 AA/AT gun mounted on a four-wheeled 60-hp Lancia Ro truck. It is probable that the gun can be used only against ground targets. The radius of action is about 150 miles.

A muzzle velocity of 2,756 f/s gives the 22.2-pound HE shell a range of 19,100 yards. The practical rate of fire is from 15 to 20 rpm. The elevation is from slightly below horizontal to 85 degrees, and the traverse, 360. An AP shell of unknown weight is reported to penetrate 4.41 inches of plate on a 30-degree slope at 500 yards, and 5.63 inches of plate at the vertical. At 2,000 yards, the respective penetrations are 3.15 and 4.13 inches.

Similar to shrapnel, for close range.

(5) 90/53 AA/AT Gun on a Tank Chassis

It has been reported that the 90/53 gun is now found on a mount of entirely new design in the center of what appears to be a tank chassis, firing forward, with a 40-degree traverse. The muzzle is said to slightly overhang the front of the chassis. The chassis itself is stated to be identical with that of the earlier M 13/40 medium tank as regards suspension, armor, and appearance, but the engine is more powerful. In order to fire the gun, the tracks, apparently, have to be locked by the steering levers. Only a limited number of rounds can be carried. The crew is probably six. Whether the chassis is used for the 90/53 self-propelled gun only, or is that of an M15 tank, is at present obscure.

g. Japanese Self-Propelled Artillery

Information regarding Japanese self-propelled guns is entirely too indefinite to warrant any statement. However in October 1941, the British reported a Japanese self-propelled gun, of which but one has been seen, perhaps an experimental model. It is supposed to be a weapon of about 100-mm caliber mounted in the chassis of a medium tank. The piece is said to be long, and to have no shield. The gun may be the 105-mm howitzer, Model "91" (1931), of which the following is known: muzzle velocity 1,790 f/s; maximum range, either 11,500 or 14,200 yards; maximum elevation and traverse (both), 45 degrees. The ammunition is a 35-pound HE shell.

32. NEW SELF-PROPELLED GUN

Intelligence Bulletin, October 1943

In Russia the Germans are using a new armored self-propelled gun, which bears at least an outward resemblance to the Pz. Kw. 6, the German tank often referred to as the "Tiger." The new self-propelled gun (see fig. 1) mounts an 88-mm cannon in a fixed turret, and has an over-all weight of 70 tons. Its maximum speed is reported to be not more than 12 miles per hour.

Although the armor of the new weapon, especially the front armor, is said to be harder to pierce than that of the Pz. Kw. 6, the Russians have found the former easier to set afire. They have nicknamed it the "Ferdinand."

A Russian staff officer makes the following observations regarding the performance of the "Ferdinand" on the Orel and Belgorod fronts, where the Germans, counterattacking, used a number of the new heavy weapons and Pz. Kw. 6's as battering rams in an attempt to force breaches in the Russian lines.

During one battle the enemy assaulted our positions with 300

Figure 1a.—New German Heavy Self-propelled Gun (front view).

Figure 1b.—New German Heavy Self-propelled Gun (side and rear view).

heavily armored vehicles, among them were about 50 "Tigers" and "Ferdinands." While the battle was taking place along our forward positions, 12 of our own heavy self-propelled guns remained hidden in their earth fortifications. When about, 20 "Tigers" and "Ferdinands" broke through our forward lines, our self-propelled artillery moved out from their concealed positions in order to fire by direct laying. An ambush was prepared near the threatened area, and the pieces were camouflaged.

Fire against the German armor was commenced when the attacking vehicles were about 500 yards away from our cannon.

Our first rounds were successful. At 500 yards "Tigers" suffered gaping holes in their turret armor and side armor. At 300 yards we pierced their frontal armor, and blew their turrets clean off. Hits on the side armor at this range nearly split the vehicles in half. It was somewhat different with the "Ferdinands." Their armor—the front armor, in particular—was more difficult to pierce, but their tracks, suspension, and side and turret, armor were no harder to damage and destroy than those of the "Tigers." The Germans lost at total of 12 "Tigers" and six "Ferdinands."

In another battle the same heavy armor of the enemy was engaged by our ordinary medium artillery, which used both special and regular ammunition. Three of our pieces were emplaced to form a triangle; they were reasonably far apart. This triangular disposition permitted unusually effective fire against "Ferdinands." Although the "Ferdinand's" fire is very accurate, its fixed turret does not permit it to shift its fire rapidly. When the gun is caught in a triangle, it is virtually helpless, because while it engages one cannon the other two take pot-shots at its vulnerable points. If the piece directly in front of a "Ferdinand" does not disclose its position by firing, the other two can usually dispose of the big gun with no loss to ourselves.

Obviously it is not always possible for us to arrange a battery in a triangle. Therefore, we require the closest possible cooperation between the pieces of a battery and also between neighboring batteries.

Point-blank fire from our medium tanks in ambush armed only with the 45-mm cannon, has taken care of many "Tigers" and "Ferdinands," as have land mines, Molotov cocktails, and cannon fire from our fighter planes.

It is also reported that the circular hole in the rear of the "Ferdinand's" fighting compartment is extremely vulnerable. This hole provides room for the recoil and the ejection of shells. Russian observers state that grenades or Molotov cocktails thrown into this opening can put the vehicle out of action.

Note: As the Intelligence Bulletin goes to press, further information regarding the "Ferdinand" has been made available.

It is reported that the crews consist of six men: A gun commander (usually a lieutenant, who is either a tank man or in artilleryman), a gunner, a driver-mechanic, a radio operator, and two additional gun crew members.

"Ferdinands" are organized in battalions called "Heavy Tank-Destroyer Battalions." Each battalion consists of three gun companies, a headquarters company, a repair company. and a transport column. Each gun company consists of three platoons of four guns each. The company headquarters has three guns, making a total of 14 guns per company. The battalion headquarters company has two guns, a Pz. Kw. 3, and four motorcycles.

On the offensive, the battalion moves in two echelons. The first echelon consists of two companies abreast, with each company in line and with a 100-yard interval between guns. The second echelon consists of the third company, also in line. The distance between echelons has not been reported.

Although the gun itself is excellent, the mounting has certain pronounced defects.

(1) The gun can fire only to the front, and is effective only when stationary.

(2) Poor vision from the fighting compartment allows more maneuverable tanks and antitank weapons to get in close to the gun

33. GERMAN AIR SUPPORT OF TANKS IN AFRICA

Tactical and Technical Trends, No. 24, May 6th 1943

GAF air commands normally detail air liaison officers (Fliegerverbindungsoffiziere, or "Flivos") to the headquarters of Army divisions and higher units, to ensure that army requests for air support and air reconnaissance are properly transmitted to the air headquarters concerned.

However, the experience in the Libyan campaigns indicated that properly coordinated air support of armored units required the assignment of a GAF officer to armored combat echelons below division headquarters. Such an officer must be an experienced pilot, capable of rapidly estimating the weight of air attack necessary to support a particular field operation, and capable of directing the concentration of this attack on any given target at the moment which the tank commander determines to be most advantageous.

In this way, air strength can be utilized to its maximum effectiveness, avoiding the dispatch of large formations to deal with small targets or of insufficient numbers to cover large and scattered objectives. During an attack against a moving target, a liaison officer with flying experience can best direct the aircraft. He controls them by radio from a vantage point where he can watch, and if necessary, follow up the target.

In Tunisia, up to December, 1942, the GAF liaison officer had not operated directly with the armored combat echelons, but had been depending on information supplied by the commanders of subordinate armored units. Since this information frequently proved unreliable for purposes of effective air support, the air command decided to appoint one of their own officers for direct liaison with the combat echelons. This officer rides in a liaison tank, which operates in the second wave of tanks, near the tank of the armored unit commander.

Assuming, for example, that an attacking tank regiment of an armored division is held up by enemy resistance and immediate air support is needed, the procedure would be as follows. The regimental commander consults with the air liaison officer, and a decision is made as to the air support required. The request for air support is then transmitted by radio to the headquarters of the Fliegerführer (officer in charge of air operations in the area); this message is simultaneously received at the headquarters of the armored division. The message should include the position and type of target to be attacked, the estimated number of aircraft required, the type and height of cloud cover, and the possible opposition to be encountered.

The Fliegerführer then orders, from the airdrome nearest the scene of action, such air support as he thinks necessary, and notifies the liaison officer when the formation is about to take off. Direct communication between the liaison officer and the aircraft is established after the formation is airborne. The liaison officer directs the planes to the target by radio. If, meanwhile, the target has changed position, he indicates its new location. Radio contact is also maintained between the liaison officer, the commander of the tank regiment, and the other tanks.

Comment: The above information seems to bear out reports from other sources concerning German practice in recent operations, and as such, is considered to be worthy of credence.

34. ARMOR ARRANGEMENT ON GERMAN TANKS

Tactical and Technical Trends, No. 29,
July 15th 1943

The accompanying sketches show the armor arrangement on current models of the PzKw 2, 3, 4, and 6. These sketches are believed to be accurate and up-to-date. Armor thicknesses (circled figures) are given in millimeters; their equivalent in inches may be found in the article beginning on page 30. A question mark following some of these figures indicates that definite information is not available. Where two small figures appear in parentheses, it indicates that there are 2 plates at this point; in only 2 instances, namely on the PzKw 3, are the 2 plates separated to form so-called spaced armor.

The armament of these tanks is also shown.

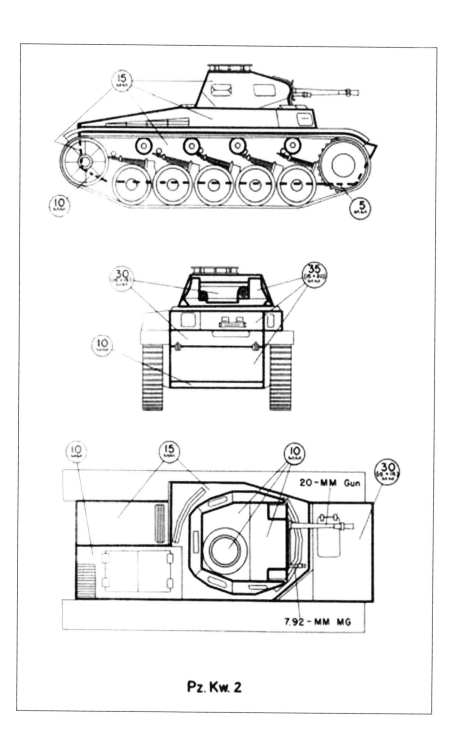

20-MM Gun

7.92-MM MG

Pz. Kw. 2

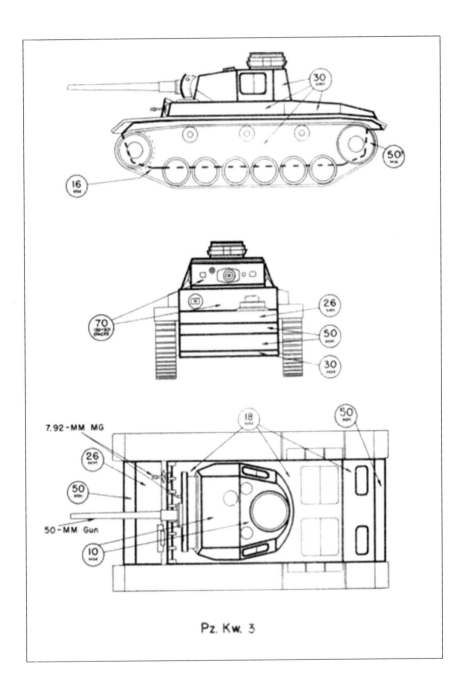

Pz. Kw. 3

134

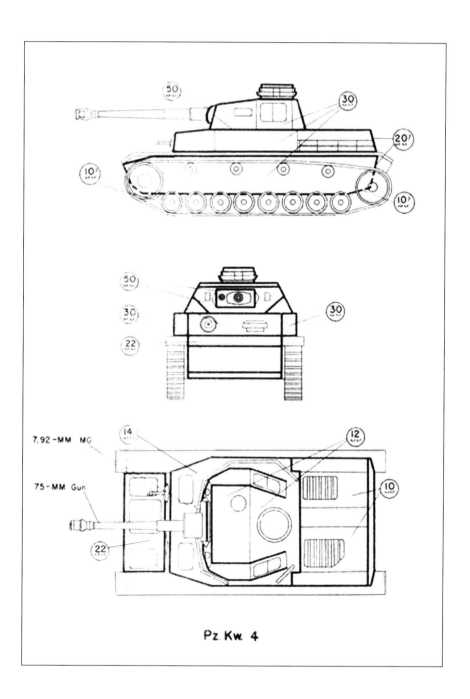

7.92-MM MG

75-MM Gun

Pz. Kw. 4

135

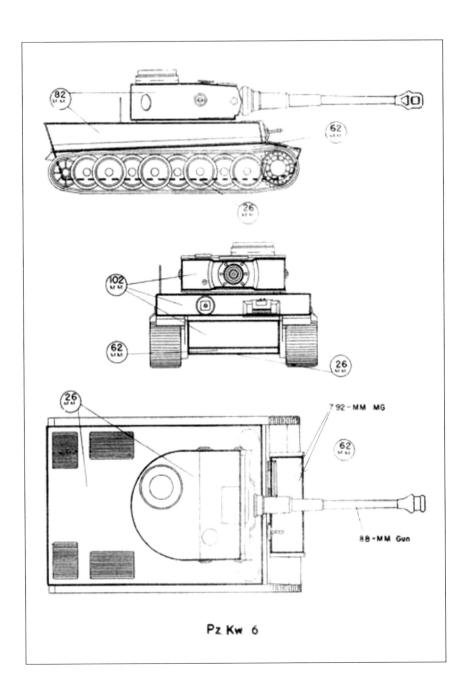

7 92 - MM MG

88 - MM Gun

Pz Kw 6

35. ATTACK AGAINST GERMAN HEAVY TANK - PZKW 6

Tactical and Technical Trends, No. 30, July 29th 1943

Construction details about some of the features of the new German heavy tank have already been described in Tactical and Technical Trends (see No. 24, p. 6 and No. 20, p. 7).

The following report by an observer on the Tunisian front furnishes some comments as a guide to training in antitank action against this tank.

It appears that the first of these tanks to be destroyed in this theater were accounted for by British 6-pounders (57-mm). An account of this action, as reported by a British Army Officer, follows:

"The emplaced 6-pounders opened fire at an initial range of 680 yards. The first rounds hit the upper side of the tank at very acute angles and merely nicked the armor. As the tank moved nearer, it turned in such a manner that the third and fourth shots gouged out scallops of armor, the fifth shot went almost through and the next three rounds penetrated completely and stopped the tank. The first complete penetration was at a range of 800 yards, at an angle of impact of 30 degrees from normal, through homogeneous armor 82-mm (approximately 3 1/3 inches) thick. Ammunition used was the 57-mm semi-AP solid shot.

"One element of this action contains an important lesson that should be brought to the attention of all AT elements and particularly tank destroyer units.

(a) "The British gunners did not open until the enemy tank was well within effective range.

(b) "In addition to opening fire with the primary weapon — the 57-mm — the AT unit also opened with intense light machine-gun fire which forced the tank to button up and in effect blinded him. His vision apparently became confused and he was actually traversing his gun away from the AT guns when he was knocked out for good.

(c) "Once they opened fire, the British gunners really poured it on and knocked out one more heavy tank and six PzKw 3s. Also, for good measure, one armored car."

The conclusions to be drawn from this action, according to the British officer quoted, are:

(a) "The unobstructed vision of the gunner in a tank destroyer gives him a very real advantage over his opponent squinting through the periscope or narrow vision slits of a tank.

(b) "The tank destroyer unit must force the enemy tank to 'button up' by intense fire from every weapon he has, including machine-guns, tommy guns, and rifles."

The size and weight of a tank such as the PzKw 6 present many problems. It has been indicated from unofficial enemy sources that extensive reconnaissance of terrain, bridges, etc., was necessary before operations with this tank could be undertaken. Bridges have to be reinforced in many cases, and soil conditions must be good for its effective operation. It can therefore be assumed that its field of operation is limited.

Reports so far indicate that the use of this tank is chiefly to support other armored units, including employment as mobile artillery. As a support tank it is always in rear of lighter units. In one reported skirmish in Tunisia, the lighter units formed the spear-head; as soon as enemy tanks were decoyed into range the lighter tanks fanned out, leaving the heavier tanks in the rear to engage the enemy units.

The PzKw 6 is now considered a standard German tank. Present production figures are believed to be at a maximum of 800 per month.

36. COOPERATION OF GERMAN INFANTRY AND TANKS

Tactical and Technical Trends, No. 31, August 12th 1943

A tank exercise observed in Germany late in 1942 indicated that the Germans were developing a new type of combined tank and infantry tactics. These tactics have now been reported as standard German tactics on the Eastern front. A description of these tactics reported through a British source follows:

Five medium tanks are drawn up in line and immediately behind them two armored troop-carrying vehicles carrying nine men each, armed with automatic weapons. The center tank leads off, followed by the remaining four tanks moving in pairs; bringing up the rear are the two armored troop-carrying vehicles. The moment the leading tanks open fire the men in the troop-carriers dismount and advance at the double in extended order. Then four very large trucks come up, each carrying about 25 riflemen who dismount and advance in three "waves" behind the tanks.

37. GERMAN PZKW 3 PHOTOGRAPHS

Tactical and Technical Trends, No. 32, August 26th 1943

The accompanying photographs show four views of the German medium tank PzKw 3. Figures 2, 3 and 4 is the PzKw 3 with the long-barreled 50-mm gun. Figure 1 is essentially the same tank except that it is equipped with a short-barreled 50-mm gun.

Figure 1

Figure 2

Figure 3

Figure 4

38. GERMAN TANK RUBBER ANALYSIS

Tactical and Technical Trends, No. 33, September 9th 1943

Analysis by British engineers of samples of natural and artificial rubber taken from the PzKw 3 tanks discloses some interesting points which are worth recording.

Two very similar articles, i.e. a vision forehead pad and a cupola pad of a 1940 model of this tank proved to be very different when analyzed. The former was made of natural rubber and was secured to the metal by the brass plating process. The cupola pad, on the other hand, was made from synthetic rubber and was attached to the metal by an adhesive paint. These samples confirm the previous supposition that the Germans have not yet learned how to make an efficient joint between synthetic rubber and metal.

The most interesting sample, however, was a section of a bogie wheel tire from a PzKw 3 tank (probably 1942). This sample proved to be made of synthetic rubber. This is said to be the first evidence received by the British authorities of this material being used by the Germans for solid tires. It seems to show that the Germans have made sufficient technical progress to overcome the heating difficulties previously arising when synthetic rubber was used for this type of work. The method of adhesion to the metal band was by means of an intermediate layer of hard, probably natural rubber.

39. NOTES OF A BRITISH ARMORED FORCE OFFICER ON GERMAN TANK EMPLOYMENT

Tactical and Technical Trends, No. 34, September 23rd 1943

In Tactical and Technical Trends, No. 28, p. 12, there appeared a translation of a German document issued in the form of a general order by the Panzer Army High Command, listing the 10 rules on the function and employment of tanks. A copy of these rules follows:

1. The tank is a deciding weapon in battle. Therefore, employment should be limited to the "main effort" in suitable terrain.

2. The tank is not an individual fighting weapon. The smallest unit is the tank platoon; for larger missions, the tank company.

3. The tank is not an infantry support weapon. It breaks into and through the enemy line, for the closely following infantry.

4. The tank can take a piece of terrain and clear it, but it cannot hold it. This is an infantry mission, supported by infantry heavy weapons, antitank guns, and artillery.

5. The tank is not to be employed as artillery, which fights the enemy for an extended period from one position. The tank fights while moving with short halts for firing.

6. The mission of the infantry is to pin down enemy defensive weapons, and to follow the tank attack closely in order to exploit completely the force and morale effect of that attack.

7. The mission of the artillery is to support the tank attack by fire, to destroy enemy artillery, and to follow closely the rapidly advancing tank attack. The main task of the artillery support is continuous flank protection.

8. The mission of the tank destroyers is to follow the tank

attack closely and to get into the battle immediately when tank fights tank.

9. The mission of the combat engineers is to clear minefields and to open gaps under tank, infantry, and artillery protection, in order to enable the continuation of the tank attack.

10. The tank is blind and deaf at night. It is then the mission of the infantry to protect the tanks.

It is interesting to report here the following notes by GHQ, Middle East Forces, based on a report by an experienced armored force officer, which reviews the points presented in the German document.

(1) It is considered that, with the exception of No.'s 2 and 3, the "Ten Commandments" are sound common sense, based on elementary and fundamental principles.

(2) No. 2, however, is interesting, since it reflects the opinions of von Arnim, von Thoma and Stumme (now all prisoners of war) who fought in Russia, where they acquired the habit of using their tanks in "penny packets".

A platoon is 5 tanks, and a company is 17 PzKw 3s, 18 PzKw 4s or 8 PzKw 6s.

Rommel would never have agreed to the company being split, and would normally have preferred to use the battalion, or even the regiment, as the unit of attack, as we would ourselves.

(3) No. 3 is debatable. Against weak antitank defense and no mines, this rule would be true. Medenine* showed that now since we are as well equipped with antitank guns as the Germans, they will have to rewrite this Commandment, and use their tanks in a similar manner to their recent employment by Eighth Army.

(4) It is interesting to note that in No. 8 the main antitank weapon is considered to be the tank-hunting platoon and NOT the tank. This accords with our own views but in the past has not been always understood.

*In the Mareth Line region

40. DETAILED REPORT ON THE GERMAN "TIGER" PZKW 6

Tactical and Technical Trends, No. 34, September 23rd 1943

In the early part of 1943 there were repeated reports of a new German heavy tank (Tactical and Technical Trends, No. 18, page 6) and as the campaign in North Africa proceeded, more definite information became available (Tactical and Technical Trends, No. 20, page 7; No. 24, page 6; No. 30, page 7). The following information is taken from a special report compiled in North Africa after extensive tests on one carefully salvaged PzKw 6 and parts of ten others scattered about the battle area.

a. Structure and Layout

The dimensions are more or less as previously reported, except for the overall width, which is 11 feet 9 inches and not 12 feet 8 inches as has been stated. The hull is entirely welded. The hull dimensions are:

- Width to outside of 28 1/2-inch tracks - 11 ft 9 in
- Width of hull at top - 10 ft 3 1/2 in
- Width of hull at nose - 6 ft 4 in
- Length from nose-plate to silencer - 20 ft 7 1/2 in
- Length track on ground - 12 ft 3 in
- Height from ground to hull top - 5 ft 8 in
- Height from ground to highest point on cupola - 9 ft 6 1/2 in
- Height from ground to top of wading air intake - 15 ft 5 1/2 in
- Height from ground to sprocket center - 2 ft 3 1/2 in
- Belly clearance - 1 ft 3 in
- Height from floor to turret roof - 5 ft 2 in

The turret is made up of a horse-shoe-shaped wall with the circular part at the back. The turret bearing is of the vertical type with the stationary race inside and the moving one outside. It is a ball bearing with 1.6 inch balls and no cage. It contains a variety of sealing

GERMAN "TIGER" Pz Kw 6
Showing air intake attachment

arrangements; besides the water seals, there is a felt seal. The traverse ring is in one piece and the clear diameter is 6 feet, 2 inches. The turret seems to come off very easily.

The turret platform is 4 feet 9 inches in diameter, connected to the turret by tubular supports. There are no basket sides. The power traverse hydraulic gear sits in the middle of this. There is a trapdoor at the loader's feet, which with the turret at 12 o'clock, gives access to an ammunition bin underneath. The turret dimensions are:

- Height from hull top to turret roof - 2 ft 8 1/2 in
- Height from hull top to trunnion centers - 1 ft 3 1/2 in
- Diameter of cupola inside - 2 ft 4 in
- Diameter of cupola hatch - 1 ft 6 in
- Diameter of turret ring - 6 ft 1 in
- Diameter of turret platform - 4 ft 9 1/2 in
- Number of teeth in ring - 204
- Width of rack (turret ring) - 2 1/2 in

The floor surrounding the turret platform is mostly occupied by ammunition bins and kept fairly free of stowage. A total of 92 rounds of 88-mm ammunition is carried, divided between nose-fuze HE and APCBC-HE *[Armor-piercing (projectile) capped with ballistic cap high explosive]*.

The layout of the crew space follows the normal German practice of driver and hull gunner-radio operator in the forward compartment, to the rear and offside of the transmission respectively, and a three-man turret, thus making a crew of five.

The 88-mm gun is slightly offset to the right side and its recoil guard extends backwards until it nearly reaches the turret ring, thus dividing the fighting space into two unequal parts. The gunner's seat is well forward and low down on the left side and the commander's seat immediately behind it and higher up; they occupy the larger of the two portions of the chamber, but both are rather cramped.

The loader, having the smaller right side to himself, has more room; the rounds of ammunition are 36 1/2 inches long and nearly 4 1/2 inches in diameter at the rim, so he needs every bit of space. The co-axial machine gun is readily accessible.

b. Armor and Vulnerability

The figures already given for armor thickness are confirmed, but there are still doubts as to the quality. Armor thicknesses are as follows:

Lower nose at 20°	4.02 in	**Driver's visor at 10°**	4.02 in
Rear plate at 20°	3.23 in	**Upper side**	2.44 in
Lower side	2.44 in	**Glacis**	2.44 in
Hull roof	1.02 in	**Flooring**	1.02 in
Belly	1.02 in	**Turret front**	3.93 in
Turret wall	3.23 in	**Turret roof**	1.02 in
Mantlet casting	3.93 in (approx)		

The side plating shows surface hardness and brittleness, with a strong tendency to crack and flake. The side plate of the turret also flakes badly on the inside.

The limiting angle for penetration of the 75-mm gun against the 3.23 inch plate is 17°, but it will penetrate the lower 2.44 inch plate at 30°.

The guns used were the 75-mm (M.3) gun in a Sherman tank and a worn 6-pounder (Mk.III-57 mm) in a Churchill tank. It is not possible to give even an estimate of the equivalent full charge. The range for the test was restricted to 100 yards. The cast armor of the mantlet seems to be of good quality, and does not break up or crack under heavy attack. None of those examined had been penetrated. The mantlet covers the entire front of the turret and there is no doubt that it gives far better protection than an internal one.

There is no protection for the turret ring other than that provided by raising the driver's visor plate 2 inches above the hull roof. This is not very effective and an additional weakness is indicated by the penetration of two 75-mm projectiles which were deflected downwards on to the hull roof from the lower edge of the mantlet and turret front.

A trial attempt was made against the front of one of these tanks with PIAT *[Projector, infantry antitank]* projectiles but they failed to penetrate either the mantlet or the front 4.02 inch plate. A German "beehive" magnetic hollow charge was tried out on the 3.23 inch side plate and successfully penetrated it.

In general, it seems that the protection afforded by this tank is very good and that for effective AP attack, a gun of the 17-pounder (3-in) class is needed. We have reason to believe, however, that the tracks and bogies, which present a large target area, are liable to damage by HE from field and medium artillery.

c. Armament

The 88-mm (3.46 in) is of the normal type with semi-automatic breech mechanism; it can use antiaircraft ammunition which has been provided with electric primers. The gun has the usual electric safety devices which prevent it from being fired if the breech is not fully closed, or the gun is not entirely back in battery position.

There is also the push button switch for the loader to press when he is ready for the gun to be fired, which completes the firing circuit and lights up a signal light in front of the gunner. The tests disclosed the following pertinent data as to the 88-mm gun:

• Length from muzzle to trunnion centers - 13 ft 6 1/4 in

- Length from trunnion centers to rear of breech - 4 ft
- Elevation - 15°
- Depression - 8°
- Length of HE round - 3 ft 1/2 in
- Diameter of cartridge rim - 4 7/16 in
- The gun has semi-automatic gear and recoil guard with deflector bag

The co-axial gun is fired mechanically by means of a pedal near the gunner's right foot. The two machine guns are of the normal type, the hull gun being ball-mounted in the usual fashion. There are three smoke dischargers on each side of the turret. They are fired electrically by three push buttons on each side of the commander's seat.

The smoke generator is lettered No. K.39. It is 3.8 inches in diameter. It is propelled by a charge of powder in a transparent plastic capsule which has a small diameter, threaded extension for screwing into the base of the generator. The charge is fired by a brass electric primer, which is screwed into the base of the discharger from the back.

Up the center of the generator, and held in place by the propellant capsule, is a tube containing some kind of igniter. The loading of these devices cannot easily be done in the heat of battle.

d. Laying and Sighting

The turret is provided with a hydraulic traverse, power driven through a vertical shaft in the center of the base junction. The gunner controls this with a rocking foot plate which gives variable speed in either direction. Maximum rate of traverse appears to be rather slow. The gunner is provided with a hand traverse which can be assisted by a second handwheel operated by the commander.

The degree of traverse of the turret is recorded on a dial in front of the gunner, and there is also the usual traverse ring in the commander's cupola. Both devices are driven off the turret-ring rack through jointed shafts.

Elevation is by handwheel geared with considerable reduction into a toothed sector. The muzzle-heaviness of the gun with its external mantlet is considerable, and a compensating spring, similar to that of PzKw 4 Special is provided.

Maximum elevation if 15° and depression -8°. The gun appears stiff to elevate but depresses quite easily. An elevation lock is provided for travelling, by which the breech can be clamped to the turret roof.

Binocular sighting is provided. This consists of two of the normal jointed telescopes mounted side by side in a frame. The eye pieces are offset from the telescope center lines by the insertion of episcopic prism assemblies, (reflecting lenses) and inter-ocular distance can be adjusted by rotating them in opposite directions. They are geared together, so as to ensure that the motion is shared equally.

e. Lookouts and Hatches

The commander has a raised cupola of the normal type with five slits backed by the usual size triplex blocks. The field of view is good. The front block has sight bars on it for lining up the turret.

There are two lookouts of the same type in the forward parts of the turret, at 10 and 2 o'clock. There are also machine-gun ports at 4 and 8 o'clock, covered by an internal rotary shield.

The driver has the usual long triplex visor-block protected by an adjustable slit. He also has the regulation type episcopic binocular. For vision to his own, the left side, he has a prism episcopic set to look about 30° forward to the side.

The hull gunner has the usual episcopic sighting telescope fitted to the ball mounting of his machine gun. He also has a prism episcope, similar to that of the driver, for looking out to the right. Both these episcopes are fitted in the hatch doors.

The hatch in the cupola and those above the driver and forward gunner are circular, about 18 inches in diameter and spring supported; they can be closed down against a rubber ring so as to be completely water tight.

There is a rectangular hatch above the loader which is also provided with, a rubber sealing ring. The size of this opening is about

20 x 14 inches. In one tank there was a large diameter escape hatch at 4 o'clock in the turret wall, in place of one of the pistol ports.

f. Amphibious Characteristics

The tank has been initially designed for total immersion in water. All the crew's hatches are provided with rubber seals and multiple bolts. The engine compartment can also be sealed off; its cover is normally screwed down on to sealing strips and it can be isolated from the radiator and fan compartments on either side of it, drawing air from a special intake pipe over the engine hatch, the top of which is 3 3/4 inches internal diameter and 15 1/2 feet from the ground, (see sketch).

No attempt is made to plug the cooling air inlets and outlets, so that the radiators run totally submerged, the fans being disconnected by special clutches. The only other aperture required is for the exhaust and this is dealt with by a simple flap-valve on top of the silencer, which is normally held open.

A free translation of an instruction plate inside one of the turrets is as follows:

(1) Lock turret and gun.

(2) Free mantlet sealing frame, push forward and secure by means of locking nuts.

(3) Remove MG and fit in sealing rod.

(4) Draw back telescopes, turn sealing stopper upwards and clamp slide with locking nut.

(5) Plug gun cradle by turning handwheel above the gun.

(6) Pump the sealing hose in the turret race up to 2.5 atmospheres.

(7) Open water-drain tube.

(8) Tighten the nuts on the vision slit frames.

(9) Open the machine-gun ports and fit sealing stoppers.

(10) Fit water-tight muzzle cap.

(11) Fit sealing cap on the ventilating fan exit in the turret roof.

(12) Close hatches.

(13) Tighten levers in commander's cupola.

(14) In the event of the sealing hose not being tight and letting

water through the drain tube, close drain tube and tighten inner sealing ring in the turret.

(15) To lay and fire after emerging, sealings 1 to 6 and 14, at least, must be opened up.

The result of this is to make it possible to immerse the tank completely, drawing air through the long intake pipe. Allowing for a certain amount of free-board and the possibility of having to climb a steeply sloping beach, operation in 14 feet of water should be practicable.

The intake pipe is in three sections, which normally rest inside one another in the hull, but can be fitted together and erected very quickly. There seems no reason why an extra length should not be added if additional depth is required.

Air enters and discharges vertically through a horizontal grating on each side of the radiator block which is isolated from the engine compartment. Inflammable liquids such as from SIP (self-igniting phosphorus) grenades, drawn swiftly through the radiator block, are not likely to do it much injury.

g. Ventilation

The engine breathes from its own compartment and therefore keeps the air circulating through it. There are, in addition, two passages passing through the sidewall on each side into the space between the fans and the radiator block. When engaged in amphibious operations, these passages are closed by butterfly valves actuated by the same lever that disconnects the fan clutches.

It is thought, that when the tank is closed down for amphibious operations, air is drawn down the long tube into the engine room and part of it is diverted through the engine room bulkhead ventilator by the suction of the fan and so ventilates the crew's accommodation before passing to the engine. The only air exit found seems to be through the engine exhaust, and if the engine stops, all ventilation must cease.

For normal evacuation of gun fumes etc., two electric fans are provided, one in the turret roof behind the loader, and one on the center line of the hull roof between the driver and forward gunner. These have ordinary mushroom type outlets, to which waterproof covers can be secured when necessary.

Radiators		Fans	
Number per tank	2	Number per tank	4
Matrix width	35	Number of blades	8
Matrix depth	20	Overall diameter	17 1/2 in
Matrix thickness	7 in	Disk diameter	9 1/2 in
Grill spacing	7 per in		
Rows of tubes	6		

h. Engine

The engine is a V-12, 60°, Maybach gasoline engine developing 650 bhp (brake horsepower). There are four down-draught non-spillable carburetors, each with twin throttle tubes and quadruple floats. Ignition is by two Bosch magnetos of the rotating magnet type, driven off the live end from positions above the rocker gear.

i. Steering and Final Drive

The principal method of steering is by hand wheel, and this operates a fully regenerative system giving geared turns of varying radius with the same sort of "neutral swing" as the Merritt Brown transmission *[One of two types of British transmission.]* In addition to this there are two skid brake levers.

j. Suspension and Tracks

The interleaved bogies and independent torsion-bar suspensions are substantially as previously reported.

Hydraulic piston-type shock absorbers are provided for the front and rear suspension only. They are mounted inside the hull, the front ones being in the forward compartment. These tanks seem to have a certain amount of trouble with their tracks; the rings securing the track pins seem to be too weak for their job. There are eight torsion bars per side, three bogie wheels are mounted on each bar. This arrangement is for the 28 1/2-inch track. The eight outside wheels are removed when the narrow 21-inch track is used.

k. Performance

It is difficult to assess the performance of this tank. The weight appears to lie between 50 and 60 tons. The maximum speed is estimated at 15 to 18 mph. The cross-country ability is also a matter for conjecture.

l. Conclusions

There is no doubt that the Germans have produced a very formidable tank, and that it must have been conceived with the idea of making beach landings on the shores of Britain. The waterproofing facilities are certainly superior in design and execution to anything that we have hitherto imagined.

41. GERMAN COMMENT ON ENEMY TANKS

Tactical and Technical Trends, No. 35, October 7th 1943

A critical study of French, British, Russian and American tanks was published on 27 June 1943 in the German weekly newspaper Das Reich. It is interesting to note that the author does not attempt to minimize the merits of American tanks, particularly the General Sherman, and that he concedes that German soldiers "know the dangers represented by these tanks when they appear in large numbers." A translation of the Das Reich article follows:

The German High Command maintains a museum of captured tanks — or one might say a kind of technical school where some of our most highly skilled engineers and a number of officers specially chosen for the purpose are testing those monsters of the enemy's battle cavalry, testing their adaptability to the terrain, their power of resistance to attack, and their special qualities suiting them for employment in attack. These tests are carried out in a forest region of central Germany where the terrain up-hill and down-hill is intersected by ravines and all manner of depressions of the ground. The results are embodied in long tabulations not unlike those prepared by scientific laboratories, and in recommendation to the designers of German counter-weapons, who pass them on to the tank factories and armament shops. The type of combat actually carried on at the front is reenacted here in make-believe encounters worked out to the last point of refinement.

The officer in charge of these experiments has developed a thesis which is extremely interesting, even though higher headquarters are not, without exception, in agreement with him. He contends that the various types of tanks reflect psychological traits of the nations that produced them.

The French have produced a number of unmaneuverable but thickly armored "chars" embodying the French doctrine of defense.

They are conceived as solid blocks of iron to assist the troops in rendering the solidified defensive front even more rigid. The Renault and Hotchkiss types of tanks have indirectly contributed toward stagnation of the military situation. It was out of the question for these French tanks to swarm forth in conquest into the plains of enemy territory, dashing madly ahead for distances of hundreds of kilometers. Their crews normally consisted of only two men each. It was impossible for these tanks to cooperate as members of a complex formation. Communication from one tank to another was limited to the primitive method of looking through peepholes in these cells of steel.

The French still have, from the period shortly after the first World War, a 72-ton dreadnaught, the weight of which is distributed over the length of three to four railroad undertrucks; it carries a crew of thirteen; but its armor is of a type that simply falls apart like so much tin under fire from a modern cannon. As late as 1940 there were those in France who demanded increasing numbers of these rolling dry-land ships and wanted them to be of stronger construction than ever before. But German troops encountered these 72-ton tanks only in the form of immobile freight shipments not yet unloaded in the combat zones.

In the opinion of experts, English tanks of the cruiser class come much nearer to satisfying requirements of a proper tank for practical use in the present war. The name in itself indicates that the basic idea was carried over from naval construction. These tanks are equipped with a good motor and are capable of navigating through large areas. The amount of armor was reduced for the sake of higher speed and greater cruising radius. Tactically these tanks are more or less a counterpart of torpedo destroyer formations, out on the endless spaces of ocean. They are best adapted — and this is quite a significant factor — to the hot and sparsely settled areas of the English colonial empire. The English tank is an Africa tank. It has a narrow tread chain. It did not come much into the foreground on the European continent. A tank for use in Europe, apparently, is something for which the English don't show so much talent.

On Soviet territory the English tank was a failure; and it shares this fate with the North American tanks, which were not appreciated very much by the Soviet ally. These North American tanks include, for instance, the "General Stuart," a reconnaissance and rear-guard tank, bristling with machine-guns, as well as the "General Lee." Although the latter possesses commendable motor qualities, its contours are not well balanced, and its silhouette is bizarre and too tall.

This criticism does not apply, however, to the most recent North American development, the "General Sherman." The latter represents one of the special accomplishments of the North American laboratories. With its turtle-shaped crown rising in one piece above the "tub" and turret it must be regarded as quite a praiseworthy product of the North American steel industry. The first things to attract attention are serial construction and fulfillment of the almost arrogant requirements of the North American automobile industry as regards speed, smooth riding, and streamlined contour of the ensemble. It is equipped with soft rubber boots, that is with rubber padding on the individual treads of the caterpillar mechanism. It seems largely intended for a civilized landscape or, to put the matter in terms of strategy, for thoroughly cultivated areas in Tunisian Africa and for the invasion of Europe. It represents the climax of the enemy's accomplishments in this line of production. But we cannot gain quite the proper perspective until we examine also the tank production of the Soviets.

The T-34 used by the Russians at the opening of hostilities in 1941 was at that time the best tank produced anywhere — with its 76-mm long-barrelled gun its tightfitting tortoise-shaped cap, the slanting sides of its "tub," the broad cat's-paw tread of its forged caterpillar chains capable of carrying this 26-ton tank across swamps and morasses no less than through the grinding sands of the steppes. In this matter the Soviet Union does not appear in the role of the exploited proletarian, but rather as an exploiter of all the varied branches of capitalistic industry and invention. Some of the apparatus was so closely copied after German inventions that the German

Bosch Company was able to build its own spare parts unmodified into the Soviet-constructed apparatus.

The Soviet Union was the only nation in the world to possess, even prior to the approach of the present war, completely perfected and tried-out series of tanks. The Soviets had such tanks, for instance, in the autumn of 1932. Basing their procedure on experience gained in maneuvers, the Russians then developed independently additional new series, building to some extent on advances abroad, like those embodied in the fast Christie tank (speed 90 to 110 km.) of the North Americans.

Like Germany and England, the Soviet Union thereupon hit upon a tank constructed for employment in separate operational units. Groups of these tanks operate in isolation in advanced zones of combat, at increasing distances from the infantry. Only a minor tank force is thrown into action for tactical cooperation with infantry forces. Such, at least, was the idea. And in fact, the T-34 was found suited for this type of action — though in many instances only by way of covering a retreat. But even for this type of tank, positional warfare has in many instances had the result of narrowing the designer's and the strategist's operational conception to the narrower range of tactical employment.

The Soviet Union also has constructed an imitation — in fact two imitations — of an amphibian tank built by Vickers-Armstrong. Another variant of Soviet thought on the subject came to the fore when the Russians constructed a 52-ton land battleship with 3 turrets, a vehicle of quite impressive appearance but provided with walls that were not stout enough to serve the purpose. The first of these monsters broke down in the mud a short distance behind Lemberg, in 1941. After that they were found more and more rarely; and at last they dropped out altogether.

In order properly to evaluate the most recent tank creations, such as the North American "General Sherman" or the German "Tiger", one must learn to view a tank as embodying a combination of firing power, speed, and resistance or, to express the same idea more concretely, as a combination of cannon, motor, and armor. In this type of construction, the paradoxes involved in the ordinary problems of automobile body building are raised to their highest potential. A mere addition to one of the above-indicated dimensions, let us say the motor by itself or the armor by itself, is not apt to be of value.

A fast-moving tank must not weigh much, and heavy armor does not ride well. The caliber of the cannon affects the size and weight of its ammunition; and a difference in the latter is usually multiplied about a hundredfold, since tanks usually carry about 100 rounds as reserve ammunition. Taking all these things into consideration, we look upon the "General Sherman" as embodying a type of strategy that is conceived in terms of movement: it is a "running" tank, all the more since the Americans most likely expected to use it on readily passable terrain, that is on European soil. The caliber of its principal weapon is slightly in excess of the maximum so far attained by the foreign countries. It is spacious inside. Its aeroplane motor is of light weight. It is a series product, the same as its cast-steel coat, the latter being modeled into an almost artistic-looking contour, in such manner as to offer invariably a curved, that is a deflecting surface to an approaching bullet.

In Tunis, German soldiers have demonstrated their ability to deal with this tank; but they know the danger represented by these tanks when they appear in large herds. An imposing innovation is the stabilization equipment of the cannon. This equipment is connected with a system of gyros and permits even and smooth laying of the gun. This system was taken over from naval artillery and applied to the shocks incident to swaying over uneven terrain, where stabilization, of course, represents a far more difficult problem. This is the first attempt of its kind ever to be made anywhere.

42. THE PZ-KW 5 (PANTHER) TANK

Tactical and Technical Trends, No. 37, November 4th 1943

The German tank series 1 to 6 has now been filled in with the long-missing PzKw 5 (Panther) a fast, heavy, well-armored vehicle mounting a long 75-mm gun. It appears to be an intermediate type between the 22-ton PzKw 4 and the PzKw 6 (Tiger) tank. The Panther has a speed of about thirty-one miles per hour. It approximates (corresponds roughly to) our General Sherman, a tank which evoked complimentary comment in the Nazi press.

The following is a description of the tank: (It should be noted that practically all data contained in this report come from Russian sources).

The 75-mm gun is probably the new Pak. 41 AT gun with a muzzle velocity of 4,000 foot-seconds. The estimated armor penetration at 547 yards is 4.72 inches, and the life of the barrel from 500 to 600

THE PzKw 5 (PANTHER) TANK

Weight	45 tons
Crew	5
Armament	75-mm (2.95 in) gun, long barrel, (1943) 1 machine gun, MG-42, 7.92-mm
Ammunition	75 rounds (AP & HE)
Cooling system	water
Ignition	magneto
Armor	front of turret and cannon shield 100 mm (3.94 in) upper front plate 85 mm (3.45 in) 57° inclination lower front plate 75 mm (2.95 in) 53° inclination side and rear plate 45 mm (1.78 in) top of turret & tank and bottom of tank 17 mm (.67 in)
width	11 ft 8 in (same as the PzKw 6)
length	22 ft 8 in (1 1/2 ft longer than the PzKw 6)
clearance	1 ft 8 in (10 cm)(3.9 in) more than the PzKw 6)
Caterpillar section	drive sprockets at front rear idlers 8 double rubber-tired bogie wheels 850 mm (33.46 in) in diameter on either side torsion suspension system hydraulic shock absorbers located inside tank metal caterpillar tread 660 mm (25.62 in) wide
Maximum speed	50 km hr. (approx. 31 mph)
Range	170 km (approx. 105 miles)

rounds. The gun has direct sights to 1,500 meters or 1,640 yards. The 75-mm has an overall length of 18 feet 2 inches.

The Panther can also be easily converted for fording deep streams by attaching a flexible tube with float to the air intake. There is a special fitting in the top rear of the tank for attaching this tube.

Although provided with smaller armor and armament than the 6, the Panther has the same motor, thus giving it higher speed and maneuverability. This tank is also provided with light armor plate (not shown in the sketch) 4 to 6 millimeters thick along the side just above the suspension wheels and the inclined side armor plate.

Panther tanks are organized into separate tank battalions similar to the Tiger tanks. Many of these tanks have been used by the Germans during the July and August battles. The Russians state that this tank, although more maneuverable, is much easier to knock out than the PzKw 6. Fire from all types of rifles and machine guns directed against the peep holes, periscopes and the base of the turret and gun shield will blind or jam the parts. High-explosives and armor-piercing shells of 54-mm (2.12 in) caliber or higher, at 800 meters (875 yds) or less, are effective against the turret. Large caliber artillery and self-propelled cannon can put the Panther out of action at ordinary distances for effective fire. The inclined and vertical plates can be pierced by armor-piercing shells of 45 mm (1.78 in) caliber or higher. Incendiary armor-piercing shells are especially effective against the gasoline tanks and the ammunition located just in the rear of the driver.

The additional 4 to 6 mm (.157 to .236 in) armor plate above the suspension wheels is provided to reduce the penetration of hollow-charge shells but the Russians state that it is not effective. Antitank grenades, antitank mines and "Molotov cocktails" are effective against the weak bottom and top plates and the cooling and ventilating openings on the top of the tank just above the motor.

This tank is standard but the quantity and rate of production is not known.

43. GERMAN 128-MM SP GUN

Tactical and Technical Trends, No. 39, December 2nd 1943

A brief and not too satisfactory account of a brand-new, rather mobile, German 128-mm SP gun has been supplied by an allied source. The gun-caliber is a newcomer in the list of German artillery, and appears to be one of the ultra-modern long weapons which have been recently turned out by the Rheinmetall Company. No specifications are yet available concerning it.

Present data indicate the gun-and-mount assembly is an improvement on the rather cumbersome, 70-ton "Ferdinand", which mounts only an 88-mm (3.46 in) weapon rather than the new 128-mm (5.03 in) piece, and carries massive hull armor running from 4.33 to 7.87 inches (see Tactical and Technical Trends No. 35, p. 16) — a plating heavier than that carried at sea by most heavy naval cruisers. The hull armor on the 128-mm gun varies from 30 to 45 millimeters (1.18 to 1.38 in) over the fighting compartment and 15 to 30

GERMAN 128-MM SELF-PROPELLED GUN

millimeters (.59 to 1.18 in) on the lengthened PzKw 3 hull and chassis. The weight is thereby cut to about 35 tons and the speed has been stepped up from the 6 to 9 mph of the "Ferdinand" to about 15.5. Whether the added mobility is justified at the cost of stripping down the armor to a thickness that may be pierced by many small-caliber antitank guns is an open question, and is certainly a reversal of trend. Perhaps "Ferdinand" was too massive to be thoroughly practical in mobile warfare. It is believed that the "128" may be used for the most part against fixed fortifications, in which case protection would be supplied by other means, which is further indicated by the fact that no machine gun is reported as part of the equipment. Only 18 rounds of separate-loading ammunition are carried. While the type of shell is not yet reported, mixed AP and anticoncrete projectiles may be expected. The crew is five.

44. POWERED ARTILLERY

Recognition Journal, September 1944

Many German self-propelled guns are modified captured material

German self-propelled guns have increased in importance with the Wehrmacht's withdrawal on all fronts. Retreating German armored divisions have left behind hundreds of these mobile assault and antitank guns.

Last December the Journal published pictures of the principal German self-propelled guns. These and many others have since confronted the Allies in the U.S.S.R., Italy and France. Some of the guns that we captured in Tunisia have continued to appear in large numbers in Europe. They include the 75-mm. and 105-mm. assault

German medium assault gun is a thick-barreled 105-mm. gun mount on the chassis of the PzKw III tank. This weapon looks almost exactly like the 75-mm. Sturmgeschütz

This captured Czech PzKw 38 chassis that mounts a 75-mm. is a favorite German self-propelled weapon. The gun is housed in a tall, open-topped, slant-sided shield well to the rear.

To pierce the Gustav Line, the Allied troops had to beat their way past many 75-mm. self-propelled assault guns on PzKw III chassis. These last-ditch defenders made the going tough for the Allies. A squat forward superstructure has replaced the PzKw III turret. It is closed in on top and welded to the chassis. Here on the right and to the left rear are views of the Sturmgeschütz.

More familiar version of German 75-mm. gun on the Czech chassis has cone-shaped gun housing set well forward. Czech suspension has short wheel base of four large bogies.

guns on the PzKw III chassis, the 75-mm. on the Czech PzKw 38 chassis and on the French Lorraine chassis.

Soviet troops first encountered the self-propelled 88-mm. gun, Ferdinand, in 1943; U.S. and British troops met it in Italy. How they dealt with the 72-ton monster is shown on page 14. Ferdinand remains the only German self-propelled gun that was made to order

Hotchkiss 39 tank with a captured 47-mm. gun is another instance of German-used French equipment. German ingenuity salvaged the weapon's usefulness. Hotchkiss 39 suspension consists of two and a half pairs of bogie wheels with "wheel pants" and two return rollers.

from start to finish — an original design. The others have all been adaptations.

The newest German SP guns continue to be adaptations of present equipment. They illustrate a trend toward greater firepower on PzKw IV and VI chassis.

45. USE OF TANKS WITH INFANTRY

Intelligence Bulletin, December 1943

1. INTRODUCTION

The correct and incorrect ways of using infantry with tanks, according to the German Army view, are summarized in an enemy document recently acquired. In this document the Germans list the correct and incorrect methods side by side. The document is of special value and interest, not only because the text headed "Right" indicates procedures approved by the enemy, but because there are implications, in the text headed "Wrong," of certain errors that German units may have made from time to time. Extracts from the document follow.

2. THE DOCUMENT

a Attack

(1) Wrong Attack not thoroughly discussed in advance.

Right Thorough discussions of reconnaissance and terrain will take place. Riflemen and tanks will maneuver jointly as much as possible, in advance.

(2) Wrong Inadequate coordination between armored and artillery units.

Right The mission of protecting armored elements not yet discovered by hostile forces will be distributed among artillery. (Flanks will be screened by smoke.)

(3) Wrong Failure of armored cars and tanks to maneuver jointly in advance.

Right Armored cars used for observation will maneuver with tanks before an intended attack.

(4) Wrong Distribution of too many tanks in proportion to infantry used in the attack.

Right Tanks not intended for use in an attack will be kept outside the range of hostile fire.

(5) Wrong Tanks deployed and distributed among small units.

Right For effective results, available tanks—at least an entire company—will be combined for the assault.

(6) Wrong The use of tanks in unreconnoitered terrain when speed is essential.

Right Terrain must be reconnoitered, especially when an attack at great speed is contemplated. Facilities for mine clearance must be at hand. If a tank detonates a mine, the remaining tanks must halt while the minefield is reconnoitered. After this, the minefield must either be cleared or bypassed.

(7) Wrong All tank commanders absent on reconnaissance.

Right A number of tank commanders must always with the company.

(8) Wrong Tanks launched without a clear statement of their mission.

Right The mission of tanks will be widely understood.

(9) Wrong When a sector full of tank obstacles has been taken, tanks are ordered to cross this sector in front of the riflemen.

Right Riflemen cross the sector first and create passages, while the tanks provide covering fire from positions on slopes.

(10) Wrong Tanks advance so rapidly that riflemen are unable to follow.

Right Tanks advance only a short distance at a time. Riflemen advance with the tanks.

(11) Wrong When two successive objectives have been taken, tanks ignore the possible presence of hostile forces in areas between these objectives, even though an attack on still another objective is not contemplated at the moment.

Right When two successive objectives have been taken, the entire area between them must be made secure by means of tanks, artillery, assault guns or antitank guns, and heavy weapons.

(12) Wrong Tanks within sight of positioned hostile tanks advance without benefit of covering fire.

Right Responsibility for covering fire is divided among artillery or heavy antitank guns. If these are not available, Pz. Kw. 3's and Pz. Kw. 4's provide protection.

(13) Wrong Tanks are ordered to hold a captured position, even though heavy weapons are available for this purpose.

Right As soon as an objective has been taken, tanks are withdrawn and are kept in readiness for use as an attacking reserve or in the preparation of a new attack.

(14) Wrong Riflemen and light machine guns remain under cover during own attack.

Right Riflemen and machine guns cover the antitank riflemen, who have the mission of destroying hostile tanks which may attempt to bypass.

(15) Wrong Tanks take up positions so close to hostile forces that early discovery is inevitable.

Right If possible, tanks take up positions outside the range of hostile artillery fire. Tanks which are compelled to take up positions in the vicinity of hostile forces do so as late as possible, so that the hostile forces will not have time to adopt effective countermeasures.

(16) Wrong Tanks remain inactive when a mission has been completed.

Right When a mission has been completed, tanks promptly receive orders as to what they are to do next.

b. Defense

(1) Wrong Distribution of tanks along the entire front.

Right All available tanks are kept together so that during an enemy attack prompt action can be taken against an advantageous point. Tanks, assault guns, and heavy antitank guns must be kept at a distance while firing positions are being prepared.

(2) Wrong Subordination of tanks to small infantry units for the purpose of static defense.

Right When tanks have fulfilled their task they are withdrawn behind the main line of resistance, and are kept in readiness for further action.

(3) Wrong After repulsing an attack, tanks remain in the positions from which they last fired.

Right After repulsing an attack, tanks move to alternate positions as soon as heavy arms or riflemen have taken over the responsibility of delivering covering fire.

(4) Wrong As hostile tanks approach, own tanks advance, having failed to take up advantageous firing positions beforehand.

Right A firing front is created at a tactically advantageous point in the area against which the attack is directed. Tanks deliver surprise fire—from positions on reverse slopes, if possible.

(5) Wrong Tanks which have no armor-piercing weapons are sent into battle against hostile tanks.

Right Tanks without armor-piercing weapons are kept back, and are used for antiaircraft protection, as well as in establishing communications and in supplying ammunition.

(6) Wrong When hostile tanks approach, German riflemen and their heavy arms remain under cover, and leave the fighting against tanks with infantry to own tanks, assault guns, and antitank guns exclusively.

Right All arms take part in defense against hostile tanks. Infantry accompanying the tanks are kept somewhat apart, however, so that tanks, assault guns, and antitank guns are free to engage the hostile tanks.

(7) Wrong All available tank reserves are compelled to remain out of action because of minor defects.

Right Repairs will be arranged in such a manner that a number of tanks are always ready for action.

(8) Wrong Tanks which must remain in forward positions do not dig in, and thereby constitute targets for hostile artillery.

Right Tanks which are within range of hostile observation must be dug in as fast as possible. In winter, they must be hidden behind snow walls.

c. Notes on Use of Ammunition

(1) Wrong When only a few hostile tanks attack, fire is opened early.

Right When only a few enemy tanks attack, it is best to wait until they are within a favorable distance and then destroy them with as few rounds as possible.

(2) Wrong Against a superior number of tanks, fire is opened at close range.

Right Fire is opened early on a superior number of tanks, to force them to change direction. High-explosive shells are used at first. Since the early opening of fire give away own positions, new positions must be taken up.

(3) Wrong Pz. Kw. 4's will fire hollow-charge ammunition at ranges of more than 750 yards.

Right Tanks which are short of 75-mm armor-piercing shells must allow a hostile force to approach to a position within a range of 750 yards.

d. Peculiarities of Winter Fighting

(1) Wrong Tanks are placed outside "tank shelters" when these shelters are being used for other purposes.

Right "Tank shelters" are to be kept for the exclusive use of tanks, assault guns, and mounted antitank guns.

(2) Wrong In deep snow, tanks do not advance on roads.

Right In deep snow, tanks keep to roads. An adequate number of men are detailed to assist if fresh snow falls.

(3) Wrong Winter quarters are located so far from the scene of action that the tanks, if required, may arrive too late.

Right When action in appreciably distant places is under consideration, arrangements must be made for the smaller units—if possible, never less than a platoon—to reach the scene of action at the proper time.

(4) Wrong When "tank shelters" are snowed under, departure is possible only after hours of extra labor.

Right Paths leading from "tank shelters" to the nearest roads are kept cleared. Snow fences are provided for exits. Readiness of tanks is always assured.

(5) Wrong In winter, tanks travel freely over roads which have not been used for a considerable time.

Right Because of danger from land mines, mine-clearance detachments always precede tanks, especially if a road is seldom used.

(6) Wrong In winter, tanks are ordered to attack distant objectives.

Right All attacks consist of a number of consecutive attacks with "limited objectives." When these objectives have been reached, the area is cleared and reorganization is completed before a new attack is launched.

46. NEW HEAVY TANK: THE PZ. KW. 5 (PANTHER)

Intelligence Bulletin, January 1944

When the Pz. Kw. 6 (Tiger) became standard, the Pz. Kw. 5 (Panther) was still in an experimental stage. Now that the Panther has joined the German tank series as a standard model, a general description of this newest "land battleship" can be made available to U.S. military personnel. Much of the data presented here comes from Russian sources, inasmuch as the Pz. Kw. 5 has thus far been used only on the Eastern Front.

The Panther (see fig. 1) is a fast, heavy, well-armored vehicle. It mounts a long 75-mm gun. Weighing 45 tons, the new tank appears to be of a type intermediate between the 22-ton Pz. Kw. 4 and the 56-ton Pz. Kw. 6. *[With certain alterations the Pz. Kw. 6 may weigh as much as 62 tons.]* The Panther has a speed of about 31 miles per hour. It corresponds roughly to our General Sherman, which the Germans have always greatly admired.

The following information regarding the Pz. Kw. 5 will be of interest:

- Weight - 45 tons.
- Width - 11 ft 8 in (same as the Pz. Kw. 6).
- Length - 22 ft 8 in (1/2 ft longer than the Pz. Kw. 6).
- Clearance - 1 ft 8 in (3.9 in more than the Pz. Kw. 6).
- Motor - gasoline, 640 hp, in rear of tank (the gas tanks are on each side of the motor).
- Cooling system - water.
- Ignition - magneto.
- Caterpillar section - drive sprockets at front, rear idlers; 8 double rubber-tired bogie wheels, 33.5 in in diameter, on either side; torsion suspension system; hydraulic shock absorbers inside tank; metal caterpillar tread 25.6 in wide.
- Armor - front of turret and cannon shield, 3.94 in; upper front

plate, 3.45 in, 57 angle of slope; lower front plate, 2.95 in, 53 angle of slope.

- Armament - 75-mm gun, long barrel; one 7.92-mm machine gun (MG 42).
- Ammunition - 75 rounds (AP and HE).
- Maximum speed - approx 31 mph.
- Range - approx 105 mi.
- Crew - 5.

It is believed that the 75-mm gun is the Kw. K. *[Kampfwagenkanone—tank gun.]* This tank gun is a straight-bore weapon with a muzzle brake, and has an over-all length of 18 feet 2 inches.

Although equipped with the same motor as the Tiger, the Panther has lighter armor and armament. For this reason it is capable of higher speed and greater maneuverability. The Panther is also provided with additional armor plate, 4- to 6-mm thick, (not shown in fig. 1) along the side, just above the suspension wheels and the sloping side armor plate.

When a flexible tube with a float is attached to the air intake, the Panther has no difficulty in fording fairly deep streams. There is a special fitting in the top of the tank for attaching this tube.

Like the Pz. Kw. 6's, the Pz. Kw. 5's are organized into separate

Figure 1.—New German Heavy Tank: the Pz. Kw. 5 Panther Tank

tank battalions. During the summer of 1943, the Germans used many of these new tanks on the Russian front.

Although the Russians have found the Pz. Kw. 5 more maneuverable than the Pz. Kw. 6, they are convinced that the new tank is more easily knocked out. Fire from all types of rifles and machine guns directed against the peep holes, periscopes, and the base of the turret and gun shield will blind or jam the parts, the Russians say. High explosives and armor-piercing shells of 54-mm (2.12 inches) caliber, or higher are effective against the turret at ranges of 875 yards or less. Large-caliber artillery and self-propelled cannon can put the Panther out of action at ordinary distances for effective fire. The vertical and sloping plates can be penetrated by armor-piercing shells of 45-mm (1.78 inches) caliber, or higher. Incendiary armor-piercing shells are said to be especially effective, not only against the gasoline tanks, but against the ammunition, which is located just to the rear of the driver.

The additional armor plate above the suspension wheels is provided to reduce the penetration of hollow-charge shells. According to the Russians, it is ineffective; antitank grenades, antitank mines, and Molotov cocktails are reported to be effective against the weak top and bottom plates and the cooling and ventilating openings on top of the tank, just above the motor.

However, it should definitely be stated that the Pz. Kw. 5 is a formidable weapon—a distinct asset of the German Army.

47. VULNERABILITY OF TIGER TANKS

Tactical and Technical Trends, No. 40, December 16th 1943

An article recently published in the Soviet Artillery Journal gave detailed instructions for the use of antitank weapons against the German Tiger tank. Vulnerability of various parts of the tank was cited in connection with directions for attack. The accompanying sketch shows vulnerable points and indicates weapons to be used against them. Material concerning the vulnerability of German tanks was published in Tactical and Technical Trends No. 8, p. 46 and No. 11, p. 28. Detailed information about the Tiger tank was published in Tactical and Technical Trends No. 34, p. 13.

A translation of the Soviet Artillery Journal article follows:

"The mobility of tanks depends upon the proper functioning of the suspension parts — sprocket (small driving wheel), idler (small wheel in the rear), wheels and tracks. All of these parts are vulnerable to shells of all calibers. A particularly vulnerable part is the sprocket.

"Fire armor-piercing shells and HE shells at the sprocket, the idler and the tracks. This will stop the tank. Fire at the wheels with HE shells. Also, when attacking a tank, use AT grenades and mines. If movable mines are used, attach three or four of them to a board and draw the board, by means of a cord or cable, into the path of an advancing tank.

"There are two armor plates on each side of the tank. The lower plate is partly covered by the wheels. This plate protects the engine and the gasoline tanks which are located in the rear of the hull, directly beyond and over the two rear wheels.

"Fire at the lower plates with armor-piercing shells from 76-, 57- and 45-mm guns. When the gasoline tanks are hit, the vehicle will be set on fire. Another method of starting a fire within the tank is to pierce the upper plates on the sides of the tank, thus reaching the

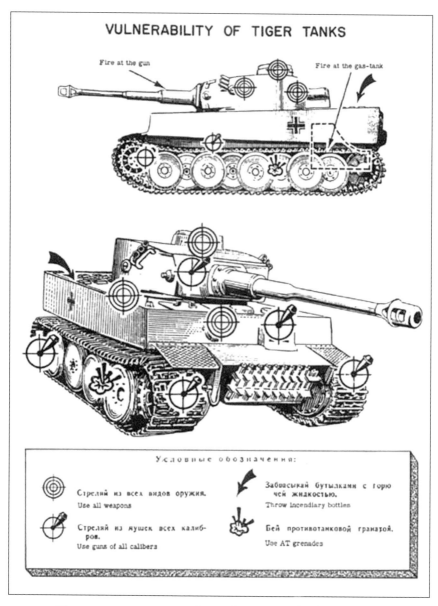

VULNERABILITY OF TIGER TANKS

Fire at the gun

Fire at the gas-tank

Условные обозначения:

Стреляй из всех видов оружия.
Use all weapons

Забрасывай бутылками с горючей жидкостью.
Throw incendiary bottles

Стреляй из пушек всех калибров.
Use guns of all calibers

Бей противотанковой гранатой.
Use AT grenades

ammunition compartments and causing an explosion.

"The rear armor plate protects the engine as well as giving additional protection to the gasoline tanks. Shells from AT guns, penetrating this armor, will disable the tank.

"The turret has two vision ports and two openings through which the tank's crew fire their weapons. The commander's small turret has five observation slits. There are two sighting devices on the roof of the front of the tank, one for the driver, the other for the gunner. Also, in the front of the tank there is a port with a sliding cover.

"The turret is a particularly important and vulnerable target. Attack it with HE and armor-piercing shells of all calibers. When it is damaged, use AT grenades and incendiary bottles (Molotov cocktails).

"There is a 10-mm slit all around the base of the turret. AT gun and heavy machine-gun fire, effectively directed at this slit, will prevent the turret from revolving and thus seriously impair the tank's field of fire. Furthermore, hits by HE shell at the base of the turret may wreck the roof of the hull and put the tank out of action.

"The tank's air vents and ventilators are under the perforations in the roof of the hull, directly behind the turret. Another air vent is in the front part of the roof, between the two observation ports used by the radio operator and the driver. Use AT grenades and incendiary bottles against these vents.

"Explode antitank mines under the tank to smash the floor and put the tank out of action."

Accompanying sketch shows vulnerable points and indicates weapons to be used against them.

48. ARMOR SKIRTING ON GERMAN TANKS

Tactical and Technical Trends, No. 40, December 16th 1943

From both Allied and German sources, reports have come in of additional armored skirting applied to the sides of German tanks and self-moving guns to protect the tracks, bogies and turret. Photographs show such plating on the PzKw 3 and 4, where the plates are hung from a bar resembling a hand-rail running above the upper track guard and from rather light brackets extending outward about 18 inches from the turret. What appeared to be a 75-mm self-moving gun was partially protected by similar side plates over the bogies. This armor is reported to be light — 4 to 6 millimeters (.16 to .24 in) — and is said to give protection against hollow-charge shells, 7.92-mm tungsten carbide core AT ammunition, and 20-mm tungsten carbide core ammunition. This armor might cause a high-velocity AP shot or shell to deflect and strike the main armor sideways or at an angle, but covering the bogies or Christie wheels would make the identification of a tank more difficult, except at short ranges.

49. GERMAN 150-MM SP ASSAULT HOWITZER

Tactical and Technical Trends, No. 41,
December 30th 1943

GERMAN 150-MM SP ASSAULT HOWITZER

In Tactical and Technical Trends, No. 25, p. 42 et seq. three models of 75-mm self-propelled assault guns were described. In issue No. 36 a description will be found of the German 105-mm SP Assault Howitzer 42. Now another and extremely powerful model of a 150-mm (5.9 in) assault howitzer, mounted on a Pz Kw 4 (8 bogie) chassis has been reported. A description of this weapon, believed to be the Brumbear (Grizzly Bear) is taken from a specimen captured on the Eastern Front, and the data are thought to be reliable (see accompanying sketch).

- Weight (probably) - 29 tons (US)
- Armament (probably) - 150-mm (5.9 in) 15-cm s.I.G. (heavy infantry howitzer)
- Ammunition - 24 rounds
- Armor: fighting compartment - 100-mm (3.94 in)
- Armor: chassis - 40 - 50-mm (1.58 - 1.97 in)
- Maximum speed - 24.8 mph

- Range - 80.6 miles
- Motor - 320 hp Maybach
- Crew - 5

This howitzer mount is designed for attacks against fortifications and accompanies both tanks and infantry in the attack. Although used against tanks also, it has not been reported as very effective. The gun is believed to be furnished only with HE shell. Additional 4- to 6-mm (.18 to .24 in) side armor plate is also provided on this mount for protection against hollow-charge shells.

50. GERMAN 150-MM SP FIELD HOWITZER

Tactical and Technical Trends, No. 42, January 13th 1944

a. General

In Tactical and Technical Trends No. 36, p. 12, this gun was illustrated in error as a 105-mm light SP howitzer. A correction was printed in No. 39, and the sketch is reprinted here with the correct caption. The gun is a 150-mm, 31 caliber medium (although the German nomenclature calls it "heavy") howitzer on a Pz Kw 4 mount. A muzzle brake may be fitted but whether or not this is standard equipment is still not definitely known. One German magazine photograph shows a group of guns which are thought to be of this type, without such brakes.

The reported German nickname is Hummel, which is translated, "humble (US, bumble) bee." British nomenclature refers to it as simply the "Bee". Another German magazine also referred to the short assault howitzer described in Tactical and Technical Trends, No. 41, p. 16, as the Hummel, although it is elsewhere known as the Brumbear or Grizzly Bear. Hummel, or Bee is probably the correct title for the 150-mm medium howitzer here illustrated. The SP-105 — l.F.H. 18 (m) on the Pz Kw 2 chassis — is named the Wespe or Wasp.

b. Description

The following are the particulars for the 15-cm s.F.H. 18 on Pz Kw 4 chassis. The equipment is known as 15-cm s.F.H. 18/m Sfl* IV Hummel (150-mm medium field howitzer 18/m, self-propelled mount 4, the Bee) i.e. the Bumble-Bee. This should not be confused with the 10.5-cm l.F.H. 18/m Sfl. II Wespe (105-mm light field howitzer 18/m, self-propelled mount Pz Kw 2 Wasp).

* Selbstfahrlafette — self-propelled mount

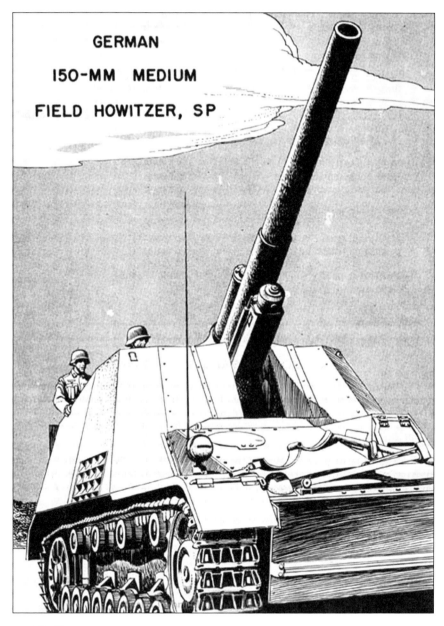

(1) Gun

- Nomenclature (German) - 15-cm s.F.H. 18
- Actual caliber - 149 mm
- Overall length - 15 ft 7 1/2 in
- Overall length including muzzle brake - 17 ft. 4 1/2 in
- MV charge - 61,020 fs

- MV charge - 71,375 fs. MV charge - 81,965 fs
- Maximum range, charge - 610,550 yds
- Maximum range, charge - 712,140 yds
- Maximum range, charge - 814,380 gds
- Elevation - 0° - 39°
- Traverse each side - 16°
- Weight of barrel - 1.96 tons
- Weight of breech ring - 266 lbs
- Weight of projectile - 95.75 lbs

NOTE: Charge 8 must not be used without the muzzle brake.

(2) Chassis

(a) Dimensions

- Length - 20 ft 4 1/2 in
- Width - 9 ft 4 1/2 in
- Height - 9 ft 4 in
- Width between tracks - 7 ft 10 1/2 in
- Length of tracks on ground - 11 ft 6 1/2 in
- Width of track - 15 in
- Ground clearance - 15 3/4 in

(b) Weight

- Weight in action - 25 tons (approx)
- Weight in draught - 25.4 tons (approx)

(c) Engine

- Engine - Maybach model H.L. 120/TRKM*
- No. of cylinders - 12
- HP - 300
- Fuel capacity - 123.6 gal (US)
- Fuel consumption roads -.79 mpg, cross country -.55 mpg

(d) Performance

- Maximum speed - 25 mph
- Radius of action roads - 96 miles
- Radius of action cross country - 62 miles
- Fording capacity - 2 ft 7 1/2 ins
- Gradient - 330

*Engine identification symbol

51. GERMANS MAKE USE OF NEW GUNS IN 'INSECT' SERIES

Recognition Journal, September 1944

In a desperate effort to cope with the mobility of the Red Army's advance the Germans have turned to self-propelled guns. In 1943 they were using several obsolete tank chassis to mount their 75-mm. anti-tank gun. At that time they introduced the 88-mm. self-propelled gun Ferdinand. Since then they have brought out a series of SP artillery mounted on the moderately fast PzKw IV medium tank chassis. This is the "Insect" series, so-called because each weapon, Bumble Bee and Hornet, has a nickname complete with stinger. In the same series, despite its name is the Grizzly Bear (below). Also in the Insect series are the Wasp on PzKw II chassis and the nameless vehicle below with a 128-mm. gun on a modified PzKw VI chassis.

Grizzly Bear here has chassis which is recognizable as PzKw IV with armored skirting. Gun is heavy 150-mm. howitzer with short thick barrel set in heavily armored gun shield. Same four-sided crew compartment appears set back farther on Wasp and Bumble Bee.

Huge 128-mm. gun displayed here is mounted on a modified PzKw VI chassis which has the usual overlapping bogie wheels and three return rollers. Gun mantlet swells from the front of rectangular gun shield with sloping top. Grizzly Bear in background is dwarfed by comparison.

The Hornet is a new Nazi weapon which adapts the PzKw IV chassis as a self-propelled gun mount for the 88-mm. gun. The engine is forward in order to provide a larger space at the rear for the fighting compartment. The 21-ft. gun barrel extends well beyond the bow of the chassis. The gun shield is tall with sloping sides. The Hornet is more lightly armored and has almost twice the speed of the Ferdinand.

German tank repair unit recovers a bogged-down Wasp from mud. Buffer and recuperator of the 105-mm. howitzer project well beyond.

Bumble Bees were part of Nazi coast defenses in southern Greece. Ventilators at side, near front of the gun housing, appear on most new Nazi SP guns. Poles near top of superstructure are flotation aids.

Nazi Wasp is refueled on Russian front. 105-mm. howitzer is mounted at the rear of the chassis within an open boxlike shield. Fighting compart-ment is open at the top and rear and has high silhouette. The flat-sided superstructure of the Wasp resembles others of the Nazi Insect series.

The Bumble Bee is the Nazi nickname for the 150-mm. heavy field howitzer mounted on a modified PzKw IV tank chassis. The gun barrel projects flush with the nose. Superstructure is a four-sided sloping shield.

Wasp mounting a 105-mm. light field howitzer is the only one of the insect series that does not incorporate the PzKw IV chassis. Packing blocks around the gun buffer suggest this Wasp never had time to fire a shot. From it American troops in Italy carefully remove a booby trap.

52. BRITISH COMMENTS ON GERMAN USE OF TANKS

Intelligence Bulletin, January 1944

In the Intelligence Bulletin, Vol. I, No. 11, pp. 53-54, there appeared a translation of a Fifth Panzer Army order signed by Lt. Gen. Gustav von Vaerst, listing "ten commandments" for the employment of tanks. This month the Intelligence Bulletin again publishes a translation of these "commandments," and adds appropriate comments by GHQ, Middle East Forces, based on a report by an experienced armored force officer.

First, the German order:

1. The tank is a decisive combat weapon. Therefore, its employment should be limited to the "main effort" in suitable terrain.

2. The tank is not an individual fighting weapon. The smallest tank unit is the platoon, and, for more important missions, the company.

3. The tank is not an infantry support weapon. It breaks into, and through, the opposition's line, and the infantry follows it closely.

4. The tank can take and clear terrain, but it cannot hold it. The latter is the mission of the infantry, supported by infantry heavy weapons, antitank guns, and artillery.

5. The tank is not to be employed as artillery to fight the enemy from a single position for an extended period. While fighting, the tank is almost constantly in motion, halting briefly to fire.

6. The mission of the infantry is to neutralize hostile antitank weapons, and to follow the tank attack closely so as to exploit completely the force and morale effect of that attack.

7. The mission of the artillery is to support the tank attack by fire, to destroy hostile artillery, and to follow closely the rapidly advancing tank attack. The main task of the artillery support is continuous flank protection.

8. The task of the tank destroyers ("Ferdinands" or other self-propelled mounts equipped with high-velocity weapons) is to follow

the tank attack closely, and to get into the battle promptly when tank fights tank.

9. The mission of the combat engineers is to open gaps in minefields—under tank, infantry, and artillery protection—and thereby enable the tank attack to continue.

10. At night, when tanks are blind and deaf, it is the mission of the infantry to protect them.

And now the comments by GHQ, British Middle East Forces:

It is considered that, with the exception of Nos. 2 and 3, these "commandments" are sound common sense, based on fundamental principles.

Number 2 is interesting, however, since it reflects the opinions of von Arnim, von Thoma, and Stumme (all now prisoners of war), who fought in Russia, where they acquired the habit of using their tanks in "penny packets." A platoon consists of five tanks, and a company consists of 17 Pz. Kw. 3's, 18 Pz. Kw. 4's. or 8 Pz. Kw. 6's. Rommel would never have agreed to the company being split, and would normally have preferred to use the battalion, or even the regiment, as the unit of attack, just as we [the British] ourselves would.

Number 3 is debatable. Against weak antitank defense and no mines, this method would be effective. However the action at Medenine, in the Mareth line area, and all action after that showed that we are as well equipped with antitank guns as the Germans are. Because of this, the Germans will be compelled to rewrite their No. 3 "commandment" and use their tanks much as our Eighth Army has been doing recently.

53. GERMAN PRISONERS DISCUSS THE PZ. KW. 6

Intelligence Bulletin, April 1944

1. INTRODUCTION

In discussing the employment of the Pz. Kw. 6, or "Tiger" tank, two well-informed German noncommissioned officers recently made a number of statements which should be of interest and value to readers of the Intelligence Bulletin. Although the material contained in this section has been evaluated as substantially correct and in line with information already known to the Military Intelligence Division, it must be treated with a certain degree of reserve, as is customary with material obtained from prisoner-of-war sources. This, however, does not alter the fact that it can be studied with profit.

2. THE COMMENTS

a. After Pz. Kw. 6's have had to move long distances, and before they can then go into action, a number of adjustments must be made. For example, bogie wheels must be changed. It is therefore unlikely that the tanks will often be sent directly into action after a long approach march on tracks.

b. Originally, it was planned that Pz. Kw. 6's should be supported by an equal number of Pz. Kw. 3's to provide local protection. The latter would move on the flanks of the main body of the Pz. Kw. 6's and cover them against hostile tank hunters attempting to attack them at close range. During an assault, the Pz. Kw. 6's would attack hostile heavy tank battalions or heavy pillboxes, and the Pz. Kw. 3's would attack machine-gun nests or lighter tanks. This method was altered in Sicily, where ground conditions repeatedly kept tanks to the roads and limited their usefulness—thereby decreasing the need for local protection. At least one battalion, which should have had nine of each type to a company, exchanged its Pz. Kw. 3's for the Pz. Kw. 6's of another unit, after which the company was made up of 17 Pz. Kw.

6's only.

c. A prisoner of War stated that on one occasion his turret jammed in turning, making it impossible for the crew to blow up their tank by means of a built-in explosive charge which was situated under one of the plates (possibly forward of the turret) in such a way that it could be reached only when the turret was directly facing the rear.

d. These prisoners remarked that in a "model" attack by a Tiger battalion, the standard company formation is a wedge or an arrowhead, with one platoon forward. This platoon is generally led by an officer, whose tank moves in the center of the formation. The company commander is forward, but not necessarily in the lead. The battalion commander is not forward, as a rule. It must be remembered, however, that the "model" attack cannot take into account such factors as variable terrain and the strength of the opposition. Therefore, deviations from the "model" formation are not only sanctioned, but are actually common.

The prisoners appeared to consider frontal attacks no less usual than outflanking attacks.

e. A prisoner stated that his Pz. Kw. 6 carried over 100 shells for the gun, "stowed everywhere"; however, the standard ammunition load is 92 shells. According to him, although the 88-mm gun in the Pz. Kw. 6 can fire up to 10,000 to 12,000 yards indirect, this type of firing is very difficult and is seldom undertaken. He declared that the best range is 1,000 to 2,000 yards—"the nearer the better."

f. Although one prisoner of war stated that the Pz. Kw. 6 carries a gyroscopic compass, he maintained that it is impossible to attack at night because of vision difficulties. Theoretically, however, the gyroscopic compass is very good for keeping direction by night and in smoke or fog.

g. According to a prisoner, the chain of wireless communication is from battalion to company to platoon. The latter link is a frequency on which all the tanks in the company are tuned, but each platoon and headquarters has a code name by which it is called up. For special operations—for example, long-range reconnaissance patrols—tanks can be netted by a frequency other than the company frequency.

However, this entails altering the sets. Alternatively tanks can be given two sets tuned to two frequencies, but this is seldom done except in the case of the company headquarters tank, where it is the normal procedure. All priority and battle messages are passed in the clear, but important tactical terms (such as "attack," "outflank," "assemble") have code names (such as "dance," "sing," and so on). Each tank carries a list of these code names.

In Russia, where German troops often were 4 miles or so from headquarters, Soviet troops made a practice of intercepting traffic between battalion and company, so that they would have enough time to take preparatory measures before company orders came through.

h. The Germans take great pains to camouflage their Pz. Kw. 6's, a prisoner remarked. Every effort was made by one particular battalion to make their tanks look like the 3-ton personnel carrier. A dummy radiator and front wheels were fitted to the front of the tank, the top of the radiator being about level with the top of the tank's hull. A thin sheet metal body was fitted over the entire tank. This metal body was supported by a metal projection fitted to the top of the turret, and was not in contact with the hull of the tank at any point. The gun projected through a hole. Apparently the camouflage body was rotated by the turret, and did not have to be removed when the gun was traversed. This rather elaborate form of camouflage exceeded the dimensions of the 3-ton personnel carrier by at least 3 to 6 feet.

54. FERDINAND AND THE PANTHER

Recognition Journal, February 1944

More pictures of self-propelled "88" and PzKw Mark V reveal details of new Nazi weapons

The Germans have been hurling their heaviest armored equipment against the Russians. Recently silhouettes and more pictures of the two newest Nazi armored threats encountered on the Russian front, Ferdinand and the Panther (*see Journal Nov. and Dec.*), have been made available to the *Journal*, are shown on these two pages.

Ferdinand is a tremendous 70-ton self-propelled mount which carries an 88-mm. gun on a chassis built to offer maximum resistance to enemy firepower. The thickness of Ferdinand's armor plate is as much as 8 in. on the front, intended to make the mount serve as a battering ram to clear the way for lighter armored vehicles of the Nazi

Lack of return rollers to take up slack in track gives motive gear of Ferdinand a dilapidated look. Chassis bow is long but gun barrel longer.

Huge bow of Panther slopes up to imposing height. turret has rounded forward wall resembling Russian T-34. Armor plate protects suspension

anti-tank battalions. There are usually 44 of these self-propelled "88's" in one heavy battalion and each one carries a crew of six. Although the mighty firepower and armor of Ferdinand make it a dangerous opponent, it has been proved to be quite vulnerable. Unwieldy and underpowered for its great size, it can travel only 12 m.p.h. on a highway and 6 to 9 m.p.h. on rough ground; to fire, it must come to a full stop. When Ferdinand is attacked by more that one opponent at a time, its fixed weapon is a great handicap. Russians concentrate their artillery attacks on Ferdinand's mobile parts which break down readily under the great weight of the chassis; also on the gun installation and on the gas tanks in the center of the hull. Grenades and Molotov cocktails hurled through a large shell-case ejection opening in the rear of the mount will blast the twin electric motors located directly inside.

A new heavy tank in the German arsenal, the 45-ton PzKw Mark V series to bridge the gap between the 22-ton Mark IV and the 60-ton Mark VI, Tiger. This tank, which is called the Panther, appears to be a first-class vehicle, fast, well-armored and hard-hitting. It has the advantage of being swifter and more maneuverable than the Tiger but at the same time is easier to knock out because of lighter armor protection. Its long-barreled 75-mm. gun with double-baffle muzzle brake is a new weapon which has a high velocity, considerable armor penetration, and direct sights up to a distance of 1,640 yd.

Like the Tiger, the Panther can be converted for deep stream fording. It has a speed of 31 m.p.h. and carries a crew of five. Its heaviest armor plate, on the front of the turret and the cannon shield, is about 3.94 in. thick. The top and bottom of the tank are lightly armored and are especially vulnerable to grenade fire.

RECOGNITION: The huge coffinlike gunshield of Ferdinand, set well to rear, has sloping sides and top. Hull is rectangular and straight-sided. Six large evenly-spaced bogie wheels support track approximately 2 1/2 ft. wide.

The Panther is built close to the ground with a low center of gravity. Its turret sides flow in sloping line into the sides of the hull. The turret is slab-sided and set slightly to the rear of center with a cupola at the back. The 75-mm. gun barrel is extremely long. From the side, the Panther's hull is sharply undercut behind. Eight overlapping bogie wheels on each side with driving sprocket in front are typical of German-designed suspension systems.

55. GERMAN TANK PLATOONS OPERATING AS POINTS

Intelligence Bulletin, June 1944

This section discusses the composition and employment of German tank platoons operating as points. Although the information in this account comes from an unofficial source, it is believed to be substantially correct.

1. COMPOSITION

The point platoon is generally made up of the platoon leader's tank and two sections of two tanks each. The platoon leader may place either the first or second section at the head of the point platoon, but he himself always stays between the two sections in order to observe his entire outfit. However, the composition of the point varies according to the situation.

The strength of the point platoon may be increased in mountainous terrain. During the German invasion of the Balkans, the point amounted to an extra-strong company and consisted of heavy tanks, assault weapons, tanks with the long 75-mm and 50-mm guns, an infantry platoon, and a detachment of engineers. A platoon of five Pz. Kw. 4's led the point. Behind them came a group of engineers, riding either on the last tanks in the point or on other tanks immediately following. After that came a platoon of self-propelled assault guns (four short-barreled 75-mm's), then the platoon of infantry riding in armored personnel carriers, and finally a platoon of five Pz. Kw. 3's. There were no motorcycle couriers.

At the historic Thermopylae Pass, in Greece, there were 22 tanks in the spearhead, but only three of these got through. A responsible German officer's comment on this was that it was worth losing the 19 tanks in order to achieve success with the three.

2. COMMUNICATION
a. Within the Point Platoon

In combat, communication within the German tank platoon operating as a point is done basically by radio. Up to that time, liaison is maintained by at least one or two motorcycle couriers attached to the platoon leader. As soon as contact with a hostile force is established, these couriers scatter to the sides and lie in ditches until the whole platoon has passed. They then go back to the company commander and report to him contact has been made. After this, he carries on by radio.

b. Within the Armored Regiment

As has been stated, there are five tanks in each platoon—two in each section and one for the platoon leader. The platoon leader and each section leader has a two-way radio; the two remaining tanks have receiving sets only. Regimental commanders and all three battalion commanders have special radio cars, each equipped with 100-watt sets. If the battalions (or companies) attack together, they have radio communication with the regiment. When they attack separately, each uses, in addition to his two-way radio (Funk Gerät 5), four sets capable only of receiving (Funk Gerät 2's). Each of these receiving sets is used for communication with one of the four companies. Moreover, each company is on a different frequency. In turn, each company commander has a two-way set and two receiving sets, and can speak with the battalion commander.

Each battalion, too, is normally on a different frequency. The platoon is on the same frequency as its company commander. Each platoon leader has his second receiving set tuned to the frequency of his battalion commander, in case his company commander should become a casualty.

If the regiment attacks as a unit, the network remains unchanged. However, if the battalions act independently, the regimental commander has no communication with them except by messengers, usually motorcyclists.

Code is used only with the 100-watt sets, from battalion up to division. During the attack, communication is in the clear, even up to the regimental commander. When battalions attack separately, however, they use code in communicating with the regimental commander.

The division commander alone authorizes messages in the clear. If the battalion commander cannot reach his regimental commander by using the two-way Funk Gerät 5 (which has a range of 6 kilometers), he encodes his message and uses the 100-watt set.

3. ON THE MARCH

a. Combat Vehicles

It is a German principle that the distance between the rear of the point platoon and the company commander must not be so great that the latter cannot see the former. It can be, but seldom is, as much as 1 kilometer. The spacing depends entirely on the terrain. All movement is made by road until a hostile force is encountered. The tanks then scatter to the sides. Even when there is danger of air attack, the tanks remain on the road but keep well apart. In mountainous country, when heavy tanks are used in the point, the method of advancing on roads is altered. Two tanks advance together, one behind the other but on the opposite side of the road.

The sections are easily interchangeable; for example, should the first section be at the head of the platoon and then leave the road to overcome hostile resistance, the second section can move to the head, allowing the first section to fall in behind when the resistance has been overcome. The Germans believe that it is of the utmost importance to keep the platoon moving forward.

b. Supply Column

During the campaign in Greece, all supply trucks were placed at the rear. In any other position they would have delayed the movement, because of the twisting mountainous roads. Any truck that was damaged was immediately shoved off the road to keep the column moving at all costs.

In more recent operations, when facing the possibility of a guerrilla attack from the front (rather than from the flank), the Germans have been known to sandwich elements of the supply column between tank platoons on the march. The important ration and fuel trucks have even traveled between tanks within a platoon.

While this plan has not been followed by a point platoon, it has been employed by the platoons following immediately afterward in the line of march. The same plan has occasionally been used by German battalions on the march, but only when there has been a danger of attacks by guerrillas or when road conditions have been so bad that supply trucks have needed tanks close at hand at all times, for emergency towing.

56. FLAME-THROWING PZ. KW. 3

Intelligence Bulletin, July 1944

The German flame-throwing Pz. Kw. 3 (see fig. 2) appeared for the first time during the early fighting in Italy. This tank is a standard Pz. Kw. 3, Model L or later, with a flame thrower mounted in the turret in place of the normal 50-mm Kw. K., Model 39, which it resembles outwardly (see fig. 1). *[Kw. K. (Kampfwagenkanone) = tank gun.]* The two machine guns, one coaxially mounted in the turret and the other in a ball mounting in the front of the superstructure, are retained.

The flame projector has a limited elevation (from -10° to 20°), while the turret has the full 360° traverse.

Fuel (225 gallons), contained in two tanks stowed internally, is propelled by a centrifugal pump driven by a small gasoline engine mounted in the engine compartment. Using fuel of the type thus far encountered, the flame thrower is believed to have a maximum range of about 55 yards and an effective range of about 40 yards. However,

Figure 1.—Pz. Kw. 3, Model L, with Flame Thrower.

FLAME THROWER ON Pz. Kw. 3

STANDARD Pz. Kw. 3

Figure 2.—Comparison of Flame-throwing Pz. Kw. 3 with Standard, Pz. Kw. 3

they have been used mainly at ranges of 20 to 30 yards.

In the flame-throwing tank, the crew is reduced from five to three. The flame thrower is aimed and operated by the tank commander, who has two pedals—the right controlling fuel emission and the left firing the coaxial machine gun. The gunner and loader are dispensed with, and their crew space is occupied by the flame throwers fuel tanks.

As might be expected, the normal smoke equipment is retained — that is, triple smoke pot dischargers on each side of the turret.

The following is a recent instance of the tactics of German flame-throwing tanks against U.S. infantry:

Two German flame-throwing tanks, together with three other tanks, supported a German platoon in an attack on a forward position occupied by a platoon of U.S. infantry. The attack was preceded by an artillery and mortar barrage which continued for 1 hour.

The tanks moved forward, and shelled and machine-gunned the position at a range of 50 yards. When U.S. troops attempted to withdraw from the sector, the flame-throwing tanks then joined the action, using their primary weapon against the personnel. In this action the German infantrymen, equipped with machine pistols, moved forward with the armored vehicles. The flame throwers were used intermittently over a 30-minute period and were reported to have a range of 30 yards.

57. SMOKE-SHELL TACTICS USED BY GERMAN TANKS

Intelligence Bulletin, August 1944

As a rule German tanks employ smoke shells to achieve surprise, to conceal a change of direction, and to cover their withdrawal. The shells normally are fired to land about 100 yards in front of an Allied force. There are no reports to indicate that smoke shells are used in range estimation.

In attacking a village, German tanks fire smoke shells to lay a screen around the village in an effort to confuse the defenders as to the direction of the attack. Smoke shells always are used to conceal a change of direction of the attack, the wind permitting. When a German tank company (22 tanks) wishes to change direction, smoke shells are fired only by one platoon. With the fire tanks of a platoon firing three shells each, the total of 15 shells is said to provide enough smoke to cover the movement of the entire company.

If a German tank force knows the exact location of an antitank-gun position, it uses both smoke shells and high-explosive shells. If the force does not know the exact location, only smoke shells are used. When a single tank runs into an antitank position, it likewise fires only smoke shells, usually two or three rounds, to cover its movements.

Smoke shells are fired from the 75-mm guns of the Pz. Kpfw. IV's [1], and also, it is reported, from 88-mm guns on other armored vehicles. Smoke shells are not fired by the Pz. Kpfw. II [2] or the Pz. Kpfw. III [3], both of which are equipped to discharge "smoke pots" with a range of approximately 50 yards. These pots are released electrically, and are employed chiefly to permit the tank to escape when caught by antitank fire.

58. PANTIGER, A REDESIGNED TIGER, NEWEST ENEMY HEAVY TANK

Tactical and Technical Trends, No. 51, October, 1944

A new 67-ton German heavy tank — referred to variously as Pantiger and Tiger II — has been employed against the Allies this summer in France. Actually a redesigned Tiger (*Pz. Kpfw. VI*), it mounts the 8.8-cm *Kw. K. 43* gun. On the basis of a preliminary report, the general appearance of the new tank is that of a scaled-up *Pz. Kpfw. V* (Panther) on the wide Tiger tracks. It conforms to normal German tank practice insofar as the design, lay-out, welding, and interlocking of the main plates are concerned. All sides are sloping. The gun is larger than the Panther gun, and longer than the ordinary Tiger gun. Armor is also thicker than that on either the Panther or the Tiger. The turret is of new design, with bent side plates. In all respects the new tank is larger than the standard Tiger.

Principal over-all dimensions of the redesigned Tiger are as follows:

- Length - 23 ft. 10 in.
- Width - 11 ft. 11 1/2 in.
- Height - 10 ft. 2 in.

Main armament is the 8.8-cm Kw. K. 43. It is equipped also with two machine guns (MG 34), one mounted coaxially in the turret and one mounted in the hull.

Armor thicknesses of the new tank are as follows:

- Glacis plate - 150-mm at 40° to 45°.
- Hull side - 80-mm vertical.
- Superstructure side - 80-mm at 25°.
- Hull rear plates - 80-mm at 25° (undercut).
- Superstructure top plates - 42-mm horizontal.
- Turret front - Approx. 80-mm (rounded).
- Turret side - 80-mm at 25°.
- Turret rear - 80-mm at 25°.
- Turret roof - 42-mm horizontal; front and rear sloped at about 5° from horizontal.

The suspension consists of front driving sprockets, rear idler, and independent torsion bar springing, with twin steel-rimmed rubber-cushioned disk bogie wheels on each of the nine axles on each side. The bogie wheels are interleaved, and there are no return rollers. Contact length of the track on the ground is about 160 inches.

59. GERMANS DISGUISE PANTHERS

Tactical and Technical Trends, No. 57, April 1945

Cleverly Imitate M10 Gun Carriage

Investigation of four German Panther tanks knocked out in the Malmedy area in the December breakthrough in Belgium revealed that the tanks were carefully and cleverly disguised as U.S. M10 gun motor carriages.

After inspecting the tanks and realizing the amount of time, work, and materials involved in order to imitate the appearance of the M10, Ordnance intelligence investigators expressed the opinion that these disguised tanks, used in the proper tactical situation and at the proper time, would have caused considerable damage.

Because the false vehicle numbers of the tanks knocked out were B-4, B-5, B-7, and B-10, investigators concluded that at least ten

Top view of Panther tank disguised as U.S. M10 gun carriage, showing hatch covers used in place of cupola.

Left front view with turret reversed. Note false final-drive housing at bottom of bow and false side apron.

similarly disguised tanks might have been in action.

Inside the one tank which was not blown up too badly to be inspected were found items of U.S. clothing such as a helmet, overcoat, and leggings. To heighten the deception, U.S. stars were painted on both sides and also on the top of the turret, the entire tank was painted O.D., and U.S. unit markings were painted on the false bow and rear.

In disguising the Panther the distinctive cupola was removed from the turret and two semicircular hatch covers were hinged in its place to the turret top in order to cover the opening. In addition, it was necessary to remove extra water cans, gas cans, the rammer staff container, and other external accessories.

The tank then was camouflaged or disguised with sheet metal, that used on the turret and upper bow being three twenty-seconds of an inch thick and that on time sides of the hull being nine sixty-fourths of an inch thick. The lower part of the false bow was thicker, possibly made of double plates. To accomplish the deceptive modifications, which pointed to at least fourth or fifth echelon alterations, the work probably was done by maintenance units rather than at a factory. The work probably was divided into four sections: turret, bow, rear, and sides.

Front view showing plate over machine-gun opening, false lifting rings and brackets, and markings.

Turret Changes

The turret was disguised by using five pieces of sheet metal, two of which were cut to resemble the distinctive sides of the M10 turret and then were flanged on the edges, bent to shape, and stiffened with small angle iron. The gun shield was carefully formed from another sheet to the exact shape of the M10 shield, and a hole was made to the right of the gun hole in the shield for the co-axial M.G. 34, a hole which does not exist in the M10 shield. Two pieces of sheet metal made up the rear of the turret, one representing the bottom slant surface of the rear and one representing the counterweight. The pieces representing the sides and rear were joined together and braced with angle iron, and the whole was attached to the turret. The false gun shield was attached to the Panther gun shield, and all the lifting rings, brackets, extra-armor studs, etc., found on the M10 turret were carefully duplicated and welded to the false turret.

False Bow

Approximately four pieces of sheet metal, shaped to imitate as closely as possible the contours of the M10 bow, made up the false bow, necessary because the Panther bow is bulkier than the M10. The false bottom was shaped to give the characteristic appearance of the front drive sprocket housing of the M10, and the top was shaped carefully and various component pieces attached to the front of the tank. All the brackets, lifting rings, towing devises, etc., of the M10 bow were also imitated. A square opening was cut in the false bow to permit the use of the bow M.G. 34, but a removable cover attached with a small chain was made for this opening.

False Rear and Sides

The false rear was made of sheet metal. It was a faithful duplicate of the M10 rear except for two holes to permit the twin exhaust elbows of the Panther to protrude.

An attempt was made to imitate the skirting armor of the M10 which appears to hang lower than the side armor of the Panther and is bevelled in at the bottom. A long flat strip of sheet metal was

Rear view showing false tail plate. Note exhausts and dummy fittings.

attached to the sides parallel to the ground, and a vertical sheet strip was attached at right angles to this strip to give the appearance of low skirting armor.

Features which aid in recognizing disguised Panthers and which cannot be camouflaged easily are:

1. The distinctive Panther bogie suspension. (The M18 motor gun carriage now has a somewhat similar suspension.)

2. The muzzle brake on the 7.5 cm Kw.K. 42.

3. The wide and distinctive track of the Panther tank.

60. GERMAN TANK AND ANTI-TANK TACTICS

Intelligence Bulletin, October 1944

GERMAN TANK TRENDS

Just what can be expected from German tanks in the near future? Which models are most likely to be employed extensively? Are present models undergoing much alteration?

A brief summary of the German tank situation at the moment should serve to answer these and other pertinent questions.

There is good reason to believe that the German tanks which will be encountered most frequently in the near future will be the Pz. Kpfw. V (Panther), the Pz. Kpfw. VI (Tiger), and the Pz. Kpfw. IV. However, the Germans have a new 88-mm (3.46-inch) tank gun, the Kw. K. 43, which is capable of an armor-piercing performance greatly superior to that of the 88-mm Kw. K. 36. According to reliable information, the Kw. K. 43 is superseding the Kw. K. 36 as the main armament of the Tiger. A new heavy tank, which has been encountered on a small scale in northwestern France, also is armed with the Kw. K. 43. This new tank looks like a scaled-up Panther, with the wide Tiger tracks. (Further information regarding this tank will appear in an early issue of the Intelligence Bulletin.)

During recent months both the Tiger and the Panther have been fitted with a slightly more powerful 690-horsepower engine in place of the 642-horsepower model. The principal benefit from this slight increase will be a better margin of power and improved engine life. The maximum speed will be increased by no more than 2 or 3 miles per hour.

Face-hardened armor, which was not used on the early Tiger tanks, has reappeared in certain plate of at least one Panther. On other Panthers which have been encountered, only machine-quality armor is used. There is no reason to believe that face-hardening would substantially improve the armor's resistance to penetration by the capped projectiles now in use against it.

It would not have been surprising if the Pz. Kpfw. IV had slowly disappeared from the picture as increased quantities of Panther tanks became available, but actually there was a sharp rise in the rate of production of Pz. Kpfw. IV's during 1943. Moreover, the, front armor of the Pz. Kpfw. IV has been reinforced from 50 mm (1.97 inches) to 80 mm (3.15 inches) by the bolting of additional armor to the nose and front vertical plates. And the 75-mm (2.95-inch) tank gun, Kw. K. 40, has been lengthened by about 14 3/4 inches.

All these developments seem to indicate that the Pz. Kpfw. IV probably will be kept in service for many months. Recent organization evidence reflects this, certainly. In the autumn of 1943, evidence regarding provisional organization for the German tank regiment in the armored division indicated that the aim was a ratio of approximately four Panther tanks for each Pz. Kpfw. IV. Now, however, the standard tank regiment has these two types in approximately equal numbers.

The possibility that Tiger production may have been discontinued has been considered. Although discontinuing the Tiger would relieve the pressure on German industry, it is believed that a sufficient number of these tanks to meet the needs of units equipped with them still is being produced.

Tiger tanks constitute an integral part of division tank regiments only in SS armored divisions. However, armored divisions of an army may receive an allotment of Tigers for special operations.

Early in 1944 a number of Pz. Kpfw. III's converted into flame-throwing tanks appeared in Italy. Nevertheless, it is believed that production of this tank ceased some time ago. Some of the firms which in the past produced Pz. Kpfw. III's now are making assault guns; others are believed to be turning out Panthers. It is extremely unlikely that production of Pz. Kpfw. III's as fighting tanks will ever be resumed, no matter how serious the German tank situation may become.

In an effort to combat attacks by tank hunters, the Germans have fitted the Tiger with S-mine dischargers, which are fired electrically from the interior of the tank. These dischargers are mounted on the turret, and are designed to project a shrapnel antipersonnel mine which bursts in the air a few yards away from the tank. Thus far these dischargers have been noted only on the Tiger, but the Germans quite possibly may decide to use them on still other tanks.

The Germans take additional precautions, as well. For protection against hollow-charge projectiles and the Soviet antitank rifle's armor-piercing bullet with a tungsten carbide core, they fit a skirting of mild steel plates, about 1/4- inch thick, on the sides of the hull. In the case of the Pz. Kpfw. IV, the skirting is suitably spaced from the sides and also from the rear of the turret. Finally, the skirting plates, as well as the hulls and turrets of the tanks themselves, are, coated with a sufficient thickness of non-magnetic plaster to prevent magnetic demolition charges from adhering to the metal underneath.

Despite the recent introduction of the new heavy tank which resembles the Panther and mounts a Kw. K. 43, it is believed that circumstances will force the Germans to concentrate on the manufacture and improvement of current types, particularly the Pz. Kpfw. IV and the familiar version of the Panther.

Evidence suggests that a modified Pz. Kpfw. II will shortly appear as a reconnaissance vehicle. Official German documents sometimes refer to it as an armored car and sometimes as a tank.

GERMAN TANKS IN ACTION

A German prisoner observes that the following are standard training principles in the German tank arm:

1. Surprise.

2. Prompt decisions and prompt execution of these decisions.

3. The fullest possible exploitation of the terrain for firing. However, fields of fire come before cover.

4. Do not fire while moving except when absolutely essential.

5. Face the attacker head-on; do not offer a broadside target.

6. When attacked by hostile tanks, concentrate solely on these.

7. If surprised without hope of favorable defense, scatter and reassemble in favorable terrain. Try to draw the attacker into a

position which will give you the advantage.

8. If smoke is to be used, keep wind direction in mind. A good procedure is to leave a few tanks in position as decoys, and, when the hostile force is approaching them, to direct a smoke screen toward the hostile force and blind it.

9. If hostile tanks are sighted, German tanks should halt and prepare to engage them by surprise, holding fire as long as possible. The reaction of the hostile force must be estimated before the attack is launched.

A German Army document entitled "How the Tiger Can Aid the Infantry" contains a number of interesting points. The following are outstanding:

1. The tank expert must have a chance to submit his opinion before any combined tank-infantry attack.

2. If the ground will support a man standing on one leg and carrying another man on his shoulders, it will support a tank.

3. When mud is very deep, corduroy roads must be built ahead of time. Since this requires manpower, material, and time, the work should be undertaken only near the point where the main effort is to be made.

4. Tanks must be deployed to conduct their fire fight.

5. The Tiger, built to fight tanks and antitank guns, must function as offensive weapon, even in the defense. This is its best means of defense against hostile tanks. Give it a chance to use its unique capabilities for fire and movement.

6. The Tiger must keep moving. At the halt it is an easy target.

7. The Tiger must not be used singly. [Obviously, this does not apply to the Tiger used as roving artillery in the defense. On numerous occasions the Germans have been using single Tigers for this purpose.] The more mass you can assemble, the greater your success will be. Protect your Tigers with infantry.

HOW TO FIGHT PANZERS: A GERMAN VIEW

An anti-Nazi prisoner of war, discussing the various methods of combating German tanks, makes some useful comments. Although they are neither new nor startling, they are well worth studying since they are observations made by a tank man who fought the United Nations forces in Italy.

German tanks undoubtedly are formidable weapons against a soft-shelled opposition, but become a less difficult proposition when confronted with resolution combined with a knowledge not only of their potentialities but also of their weaknesses.

When dealing with German heavy tanks, your most effective weapon is your ability to keep still and wait for them to come within effective range. The next most important thing is to camouflage your position with the best available resources so that the German tanks won't spot you from any angle.

If these two factors are constantly kept in mind, the battle is half won. Movement of any kind is a mistake which certainly will betray you, yet I saw many instances of this self-betrayal by the British in Italy. Allow the enemy tank to approach as close as possible before engaging it — this is one of the fundamental secrets of antitank success. In Italy I often felt that the British opened fire on tanks much too soon. Their aim was good, but the ranges were too great, and the rounds failed to penetrate. My own case is a good illustration: if the opposition had held its fire for only a few moments longer, I should not be alive to tell this tale.

By letting the German tank approach as close as possible, you gain a big advantage. When it is on the move, it is bound to betray its presence from afar. Whereas you yourself can prepare to fire on it without giving your own position away. The tank will spot you only after you have fired your first round.

A tank in motion cannot fire effectively with its cannon; the gunner can place fire accurately only when the vehicle is stationary. Therefore, there is no need to be unduly nervous because an approaching tank swivels its turret this way and that. Every tank commander will do this in an attempt to upset his opponents' tank recognition. If the tank fires nothing but its machine guns, you can be pretty sure that you have not yet been spotted.

Consider the advantages of firing on a tank at close range:

1. In most cases the leading tank is a reconnaissance vehicle. Survivors of the crew, when such a short distance away from you, have little chance of escape. This is a big advantage, inasmuch as they cannot rejoin their outfit and describe the location of your position to the main body.

2. Another tank following its leader on a road cannot run you down. In order to bypass the leading tank, it has to slow down. Then, long before the gunner can place fire on you, you can destroy the tank and block the road effectively. Earlier in the war, a German tank man I knew destroyed 11 hostile tanks in one day by using this method.

VULNERABILITY OF THE PZ. KPFW. VI

A tank is such a complicated weapon, with its many movable parts and its elaborate mechanism, that it is particularly valuable to know its points of greatest vulnerability. Recently the Soviet Artillery Journal published a number of practical suggestions, based on extensive combat experience, regarding the vulnerability of the Tiger.

All weapons now used for destroying German tanks — antitank guns and rifles, caliber .50 heavy machine guns, antitank grenades, and Molotov cocktails — are effective against the Pz. Kpfw. VI.

1. Suspension System. — The mobility of tanks depends upon the proper functioning of the suspension parts: the sprocket (small driving wheel), the idler (small wheel in the rear), the wheels, and the tracks. All these parts are vulnerable to shells of all calibers. The sprocket is especially vulnerable.

Fire armor-piercing shells and high-explosive shells at the sprocket, idler, and tracks.

Fire at the wheels with high-explosive shells. Use antitank grenades, antitank mines, and movable antitank mines against the suspension parts. Attach three or four mines to a board. Place the board wherever tanks are expected to pass. Camouflage the board and yourself. As a tank passes by, pull the board in the proper direction and place it under the track of the tank.

[A German source states that this method was successfully used on roads and road crossings in Russia, and that it still is taught in tank combat courses for infantry. The mine is called the Scharniermine (pivot mine). It consists of a stout length of board, 8 inches wide by 2 inches thick, and cut to a length dependent on the width of the road to be blocked. A hole is bored at one end, through which a spike or bayonet can be driven into the ground, thus providing a pivot for the board. A hook is fastened to the other end of the board, and a rope is tied to the hook, as shown in Figure 3. Tellermines are secured to the top of the board.

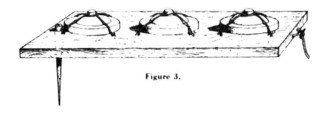

Figure 3.

One man can operate this mine. After the board has been fastened down at one end with the spike (in emergencies, a bayonet) and a rope tied to the hook at the other end, the board is laid along the side of the road. On the opposite side of the road, a man is posted in a narrow slit trench. He holds the other end of the rope. When a tank approaches, the tank hunter waits until it is close enough to the pivoted board, and, at the very last moment, he pulls the free end of the board across the road. The rope and slit trench must be well camouflaged. A good deal of emphasis is placed on this point.]

2. Side Armor Plates. — There are two armor plates on each side of the tank. The lower plate is partly covered by the wheels. This plate protects the engine and the gasoline tanks, which are located in the rear of the hull — directly beyond and over the two rear wheels. Ammunition is kept in special compartments along the sides of the tank. These compartments are protected by the upper armor plate.

Fire armor-piercing shells from 76-, 57-, and 45-mm guns at the upper and lower armor plate. When the gas tanks or ammunition compartments are hit, the vehicle will be set on fire.

3. Rear Armor Plate. — The rear armor plate protects the engine, the gasoline tank, and the radiators.

Use antitank guns. Aim at the rear armor plate. When the engine or the gasoline tanks are hit, the tank will halt and will begin to burn.

4. Peepholes, Vision Ports, and Slits. — The main turret has two openings for firing small-arms weapons, and two vision ports. The turret has five observation slits. There are two sighting devices on the roof of the front part of the tank — one for the driver, the other for the gunner. There is also a port with sliding covers in the front armor plate.

Use all available weapons for firing at the peepholes, observation ports, vision slits, and the ports for small-arms weapons.

5. Turrets. — The commander's turret is an important and vulnerable target.

Fire high-explosive and armor-piercing shells of all calibers at the commander's turret. Throw antitank grenades and incendiary bottles after the turret has been damaged.

The tank commander, the turret commander, and the gunner ride in the turret. The tank gun and many mechanical devices are found in the turret.

Fire at the turret with 76-, 57-, and 45-mm shells at ranges of 500 yards or less.

6. Tank Armament. — The turret is armed with a gun and a machine gun mounted coaxially. Another machine gun is found in the front part of the hull. It protrudes through the front armor plate, on a ball mount, and is manned by, the radio operator.

Concentrate the fire of all weapons on the armament of the tank. Fire with antitank rifles at the ball mount of the hull machine gun.

7. Air Vents and Ventilators. — The air vents and the ventilators are found under the slit-shaped perforations of the roof of the hull, directly behind the turret. Another air vent is located in the front part of the roof, between the two observation ports used by the radio operator and the driver.

Use incendiary bottles and antitank grenades to damage the ventilating system.

8. Tank Floor. — When an antitank mine explodes under the tank, the floor of the tank is smashed, and the tank is knocked out of action.

9. Base of Turret. — There is a 10-mm slit going all around the turret, between the base of the turret and the roof of the hull.

Fire at the base of the turret with heavy machine guns and antitank guns, to destroy the turret mechanism, and disrupt the field of fire. Fire with high-explosive shells at the base of the turret in order to wreck the roof of the hull and put the tank out of action.

61. A TANK-INFANTRY TEAM OBSERVED IN COMBAT

Intelligence Bulletin, December 1944

For a period of 36 hours in the last days of July, an officer of an Allied army group staff had an excellent opportunity of observing German tanks and infantry attacking an Allied force in France. The following notes, which are based on his report, describe the tactics that the Germans employed.

The general situation was fluid at the time of the attack. The Germans advanced westward in three parallel columns, each consisting of tanks accompanied by infantry. The center column followed a main road, firing rapidly and moving at a brisk rate. It went from hill to hill, with the accompanying infantry dog-trotting through the fields on each side of the road and over the hedgerows. The infantry was deployed over no more than the width of a single field on each side. The center column had a total of only about eight track-laying vehicles. At least three of these were tanks, one or two probably were self-propelled guns, and the remainder probably were half-track personnel carriers.

Although the total German strength which had been sent to capture and hold an important crossroads at St. Denisière consisted of two companies of infantry and probably not more than ten tanks, the Allied officer observed only the track-laying vehicles previously mentioned and possibly a platoon of infantry.

The Infantrymen Moved Fast

The leading tank fired its 75 rapidly, getting both graze and air bursts, while its machine guns, supplemented by those of the vehicles behind it, sprayed the top of every hedgerow. The noise was terrific, and the bursts in the shrubbery and the tops of trees and hedgerows were certainly impressive. Even before the shock of the guns discharged at close range, and the garden-hose spray of machine-gun bullets, had taken full effect, German infantrymen were over the hedgerow and into the field and were advancing toward the next field with determination and courage. They knew where they were going, and went there fast.

At night the Germans reacted forcefully, with fire and limited movement, whenever they detected any sign of an Allied approach. The German tanks moved slowly, and made very little noise. Immediately after firing, each tank moved to a new position 25 to 50 yards away. It should be emphasized that the noise discipline of the German tank crews and the accompanying infantry was superior. There was no talking or shouting; except for machine-gun and cannon fire and the starting of motor, no sound carried farther than 100 yards.

On the other hand, the approach of U.S. tanks and the passing of most U.S. motor convoys was rapidly identifiable by the loud shouting, talking, and issuing of orders by the U.S. troops who approached or passed the general vicinity of a German position. The propensity of U.S. tank drivers to "gun" their motors was a dead give-away, whereas the Germans always eased their tanks forward, traveled in low gear, and were remarkably quiet in all operations except the firing. They used long bursts of their rapid-firing machine guns to discourage guests. If pressed at all, they sent up flares to obtain German artillery and mortar fire on their flanks. The way they handled their tanks was bold and sure. They acted as if they knew exactly what their destination was, and by which route they wished to proceed.

A U.S. Tank "Got the Works"

At 0230, the darkest part of the night, a German tank moved out and headed toward the northernmost German column, making as little noise as possible. Later it turned out that a lone U.S. tank on reconnaissance had pushed up against the nose of the ridge that the German tanks had organized, and the Germans were quietly laying plans to place a terrific amount of fire on it. Before long, it got the works.

Because there were so few German infantrymen, and because they were interested only in reaching and holding the team's objective, their mopping-up activities were negligible. Thus, of the Allied troops overrun in this fashion, a large percentage was neither killed, wounded, captured, or missing during the first two or three days. The ease and rapidity with which this small attacking force made its penetration, reached its objective, sat on the objective, and cut traffic on an important road is of more than ordinary interest. Also, it is reasonable to assume that the Germans will employ small groups for similar missions in the future.

62. "THE HEAVY MOBILE PUNCH"

Intelligence Bulletin, May 1945

Recently the Germans have intensified their efforts to exploit armor, in spite of the deteriorating situation. These notes reveal the tactics of German armor at the present time.

Alarmed by the growing German tendency, early in 1945, to commit armor in small groups, or even singly, General Student, Supreme Commander of a German army group, made a vigorous attempt to correct this practice. General Student was shrewd enough to know that the reason for so much dispersion of armored equipment within his command was the very natural anxiety of his troops to obtain security in all localities. In stressing that strong measures would be necessary "to combat the tendency prevailing in the infantry to split up assault-gun battalions and tank, assault-gun, and tank-destroyer companies," Student pointed out that success is achieved only by commitment in a body—in battery or company strength, at least—at points of main effort. In effect, what he demanded was a return to normal German doctrine.

When tanks, assault guns, or tank destroyers lose their full mobility because of Allied action or mechanical defects, the General observed, it is folly to retain such equipment in the line merely so that their weapons can be utilized.

In the light of the situation then existing, he declared, "The fuel and spare-parts situation does not permit so much as 1 meter of unnecessary travel." As a result, he allowed only corps or divisions to decide on, and supervise, the shifting, routing, and other movement of tank and assault-gun units.

As to commitment, General Student ordered that if, in a battery or company, the number of weapons ready for action should drop to less than three, the unit was to be committed only in conjunction with other tank or assault-gun units until the weapons could be built up to their full strength.

"I prohibit the piecemeal commitment of tanks, assault guns, or

This is the latest model of the Pz.Kpfw. Panther.

tank destroyers," the General ordered.

Divisions which had tank, assault-gun, or tank-destroyer units assigned to them were to keep a reserve of these weapons in readiness, preferably in company or battery strength. After a commitment, such a reserve was to be restored to full strength as rapidly as possible. For security reasons, these reserve weapons were not to remain in the main line of resistance.

Of timely-value, in connection with these problems with which General Student has had to cope, is some further information from a well-informed and credible prisoner of war.

The primary mission of German tanks, as this source explains, is to provide the heavy mobile punch. This is why "piecemeal commitment" violates the basic German canon of tank warfare. And it also explains why the enemy has gone to such great lengths to increase the caliber and muzzle velocity of his tank guns. The better the gun, the better the tank, according to the German way of thinking. Machine guns play a secondary role, and are used relatively little, except against tank hunters. A hard-hitting tank that can crush steel is the equipment in which the Germans now place their faith, believing, as they do, that such tanks must clear the way for Panzer Grenadier elements to advance with their automatic weapons.

Conforming to this tactical doctrine, the Panther has a super-long

75-mm gun. Panther personnel, according to this prisoner-of-war source, are trained to engage a Sherman tank without hesitation at a range of from 2,000 to 2,200 yards. They are taught that while the preferable range of 800 to 900 yards will improve accuracy, it will not add greatly to the punch. The gun has an optical sight with three graduations: one for high-explosive shells, one for armor-piercing shells, and the third for the coaxially-mounted machine gun. Each graduation has its own range subdivision. According to the source, the gun is seldom, if ever, used as indirect artillery.

This source had been taught that, in the approach march, the tanks moved in column, covered by eight-wheel armored reconaissance cars ahead. These vehicles, he states, are part of the reconnaissance platoon of each tank battalion. If contact with hostile armor is made, the tanks deploy and attack, echeloned in depth. However, in the battle around Noville on Christmas Day, these tactics were not followed. A Captain Hingst, commanding officer of a 1st (German tank) Battalion, ordered all tanks to attack in a shallow skirmish line. The U.S. commander quickly sized up the situation, and in 45 minutes his Shermans had completely destroyed six Panthers. The Germans withdrew, and Hingst was replaced by a Captain Scheer, commanding officer of the 2d Battalion. What was left of the two battalions was combined into an improvised team. Captain Scheer then tried to bypass the U.S. center of resistance, but it was too tough a nut for him to crack.

An interesting prisoner-of-war disclosure confirms the existence of a German order to the effect that if a hopeless situation develops, and if a unit is threatened with capture or annihilation, all officers and sergeants are to withdraw and report to the next higher command. It is explained that this measure was adopted to reduce the heavy battle losses in unit leaders.

63. THE GERMAN MOUSE

Intelligence Bulletin, March 1946

Super-Super-Super-Heavy Tank Became Hitler's White Elephant

One of the subjects of liveliest controversy during the Allied invasion of France was the heavy tank — the 50-ton Pershing, the 62-ton Tiger, the 75-ton Royal Tiger. Were these worth their weight? Did they gain — in protection and fire power — as much as they sacrificed in mobility? Adolph Hitler's mind was presumably made up on this point. A pet project of his, which few were aware of, appears to have been a superheavy tank that would have dwarfed even the Royal Tiger. Dubbed the Mouse, this behemoth of doubtful military value was to weigh 207 tons, combat loaded. Two were actually built, although they were never equipped with their armament.

The Mouse is an amazing vehicle, with spectacular characteristics. The glacis plate up front is approximately 8 inches (200 mm) thick. Since it is sloped at 35 degrees to the vertical, the armor basis is therefore 14 inches. Side armor is 7 inches (180 mm) thick, with the rear protected by plates 6 1/4 inches (160 mm) thick. The front of the turret is protected by 9 1/2 inches (240 mm) of cast armor, while the 8-inch (200 mm) thick turret sides and rear were sloped so as to give the effect of 9 inches (230 mm) of armor.

ARMAMENT

For the main armament, a pea-shooter like an 88-mm gun was ignored. Selected instead was the powerful 128-mm tank and antitank gun, which was later to be replaced by a 150-mm piece 38 calibers in length. (The standard German medium field howitzer 15 cm s.F.H. 18 is only 29.5 calibers in length.) Instead of mounting a 7.9-mm machine gun coaxially, the Mouse was to have a 75-mm antitank gun 76 calibers in length next to the 128- or 150-mm gun. A machine cannon for antiaircraft was to be mounted in the turret roof, along with a smoke grenade projector.

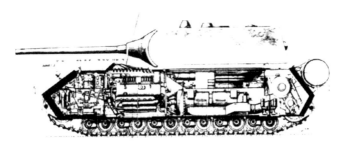

This German drawing shows a sectionalized elevation of the Mouse hull. The following salient features may be diingtinguished: driver's seat (20) and periscope (14 and 18); radio operator's seat (12) and radio (21); radio antenna (28); air intakes for main engine (30); main engine (3); generator (4); the right motor of the two electric motors driving the sprockets (9); auxiliary fuel tank (29). The coaxial 75-mm gun is on the right of the turret; its position relative to the 128-mm gun is shown in dotted outline.

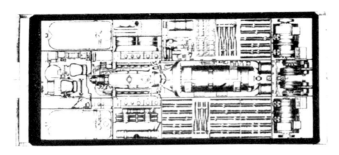

A sectionalized plan view of the Mouse hull gives another view of many of the features shown in the first illustration. The driver's and radio operator's seats (left) are flanked by the main fuel tanks. Just to their rear is the main engine, flanked by air pumps and radiators. Further to the rear is the generator, with ammunition stowage in the sponsons on either side. In the sponson on the front right of the generator is the auxiliary engine, with storage batteries to its rear. To the rear of the hull, also in the sponsons, are the motors furnishing the electric drive. The actual transmission is in the deep part of hull between the motors, behind generator.

In size, the Mouse was considerably larger than any German tank. Its length of 33 feet made it nearly 50 percent longer than the Royal Tiger. Because of rail transport considerations. its width was kept to 12 feet (that of the Royal Tiger and Tiger). A 12-foot height made it a considerable target.

In order to reduce the ground pressure so that the tank could have some mobility, the tracks had to be made very wide—all of 43.3 inches. With the tracks taking up over 7 of its 12 feet of width, the

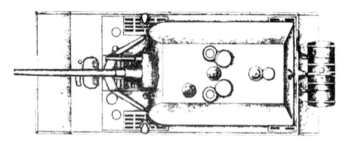

The Mouse was as vulnerable to close-in attack as any other tank, if not more so. The large hull openings were a particular disadvantage. Note their extent: the grills of the engine access hatch, the grilled air vents which flank it, and the grills under the rear of the turret, which cool the electric motors. The auxiliary fuel tank on the rear was a considerable fire hazard.

Mouse presents a very strange appearance indeed from either a front or rear view. With such a track width, and a ground contact of 19 feet 3 inches, the Mouse keeps its ground pressure down to about 20 pounds per square inch—about twice that of the original Tiger.

POWER PLANTS

Designing an engine sufficiently powerful to provide motive power for the mammoth fighting vehicle was a serious problem. Though the Germans tried two engines, both around 1,200 horsepower (as compared to the Royal Tiger's 590), neither could be expected to provide a speed of more than 10 to 12 miles an hour. The Mouse can, however, cross a 14-foot trench and climb a 2-foot 4-inch step.

Whatever the military possibilities of the Mouse might be, it certainly gave designers space in which to run hog wild on various features which they had always been anxious to install in tanks. One of these gadgets was an auxiliary power plant. This plant permitted pressurizing of the crew compartment, which in turn meant better submersion qualities when fording, and good antigas protection. Auxiliary power also permitted heating and battery recharging.

One of the fancy installations was equipment designed for fording in water 45 feet deep—a characteristic made necessary by weight limits of bridges. Besides sealing of hatches and vents, aided by pressurizing, submersion was to be made possible by the installation of a giant cylindrical chimney or trunk, so large that it could serve as a crew escape passage if need be. The tanks were intended to ford in pairs, one powering the electric transmission of the other by cable.

The electric transmission was in itself an engineering experiment of some magnitude. This type of transmission had first been used on the big Elephant assault gun-tank destroyer in 1943, and was considered by some eminent German designers as the best type of transmission—if perfected—for heavy tanks.

Another interesting feature of the Mouse from the engineering point of view was the return from torsion bar suspension—such as was used in the *Pz. Kpfw. III*, the Panther, the Tiger, and the Royal Tiger—to a spring suspension. An improved torsion bar design had been considered for the Mouse, but was abandoned in favor of a volute spring type suspension.

WHY THE MOUSE?

Just why the Germans wanted to try out such a monstrosity as the Mouse is a question to be answered by political and propaganda experts. Whereas such a heavy tank might conceivably have had some limited military usefulness in breakthrough operations, it was no project for Nazi Germany experimentation in 1943, 1944, and 1945. For not only did German authorities waste time of engineers and production facilities on the two test models, but they even went

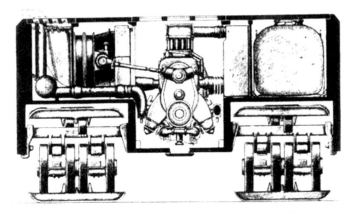

The size and weight of the Mouse made necessary extremely wide tracks in relation to hull width. This view also shows half of the engine air-cooling system (left), and rear of right fuel tank, with an oil tank just to its left.

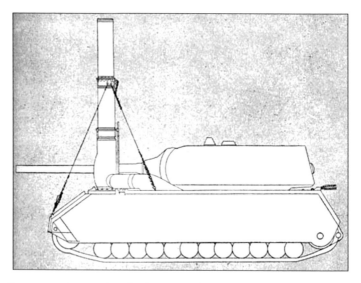

The Mouse was designed to ford up to 45 feet of water. To do so, the tank was made watertight. A trunk was fitted over the hull escape hatch, and trunk extensions bolted over the engine vents. The trunk contalned an escape ladder, and was divided into three sections, the number used varying with water depth. A second Mouse supplied electricity to the fording Mouse motors through a cable attached to the rear, as shown.

so far as to construct a special flat car for rail transport.

The drawbacks inherent in such a heavy tank are patent. Weigh not only denies practically every bridge in existence to the Mouse, but it impedes rail movement unless railways are properly reinforced at bridges, culverts, and other weak points. Fording to 45-foot depths would have solved many of the stream-crossing problems in Europe, but it seems that the Mouse could actually cross in water no deeper than 26 feet. Though sitting in a rolling fortress, the six men of the Mouse crew are practically as blind as in any tank. Because of low speed and high silhouette their vehicle would be most vulnerable to hits. Since it is reasonable to suppose that heavily fortified, static positions suitable for attack by a Mouse would also be fitted with very heavy, high-velocity guns capable of antitank fire, the even occasional combat value of the Mouse comes into question. The German 128-mm *Pak 44* (also known in modified forms as the *12.8 cm Pak 80*) is reputed to be able to penetrate 7 inches of armor at 2,000 yards. Since the Germans actually had their *Pak 44* in service in 1945, when the Mouse was not yet in the production stage, it would appear that the Germans had the antidote before the giant tanks were ready. Moreover, in the later days of the war, a rolling colossus like a Mouse would have been almost impossible to conceal, and would have fallen an easy prey to air power.

The psychological factor thus appears to have played a large part in the demand for construction of the Mouse. The German Army would never have desired such a tank, especially in 1942 when its design was apparently initiated. On the other hand, it would have made lurid headlines and Sunday supplement copy in both Allied and German press circles. But whatever the public reaction might have been, it seems questionable that the Mouse could have exerted any psychological effect on Russian, British, or American front-line troops unless the Germans possessed almost overwhelming strength, as they did when they crushed the Maginot Line in 1940. In 1944-45 it would have been too easy a mark for Allied gun and planes the first instant it appeared.

MICE OF THE FUTURE

The appearance of such a vehicle in the opening phases of a future war is not to be entirely discounted. When Red Army armored units counterattacked German forces advancing northward toward

A head-on view of the Mouse model affords an idea of the formidable appearance of the original Mice. Note the exceptional width of the tracks.

German engineers, concerned over the effect of turns upon track performance, made this electric-powered, remote controlled, large-scale wooden replica.

Leningrad in 1941, the Soviets effected a substantial surprise and just missed obtaining a considerable victory by throwing in for the first time heavy 46-ton KV tanks backed by 57-ton modified KV's mounting 152-mm tank guns in their turrets,

The first days of a war are a time of uncertainty. This is a period when peacetime armies are proving themselves, when their personnel are still anxious to determine the validity of their matériel and tactical doctrines, when they are anxious to discover what the enemy is like. Rumors grow fast, and untried men are likely to be impressed with the mere report of the size and gun power of a superheavy tank. Officers and noncoms should therefore be aware of the possibility of encountering such colossal tanks. They should see that their men know the deficiencies and real purpose of outlandish vehicles of the class of the German Mouse, and that they do not attribute to these vehicles capabilities out of all proportion to their actual battle value.

More from the same series

Most books from the 'Hitler's War Machine' series are edited and endorsed by Emmy Award winning film maker and military historian Bob Carruthers, producer of Discovery Channel's Line of Fire and Weapons of War and BBC's Both Sides of the Line. Long experience and strong editorial control gives the military history enthusiast the ability to buy with confidence.

Tiger I in Combat   Tiger I Crew Manual   Panzers at War 1939-1942   Panzers at War 1943-1945

Wolf Pack - the U boats   Poland 1939   Luftwaffe Combat Reports   Sturmgeschütze

German Artillery in Combat   Panzer Combat Reports   The Panther V in Combat   German Tank Hunters

The Afrika Korps in Combat   Panzers I & II   Panzer III   Panzer IV

For more information visit www.pen-and-sword.co.uk